Mission to Nootka

Augustin Joseph Brabant was born at Rolleghem, West Flanders, on October 23, 1845. He graduated from St. Amandus' College, Courtrai, in 1865. Largely due to having read the work of Father Desmet, Brabant felt the call to the priesthood, particularly so that he would work as a missionary among the North American Indians. He entered the American College of Louvain in 1865, and three years later was ordained in the Cathedral of St. Rombaut, Mechelen. In 1869 Father Brabant left Europe for Vancouver Island, where, except for brief trips to Europe and the United States, he remained for the rest of his life. At Hesquiat, in 1875, he founded the first mission on the west coast of Vancouver Island. In 1908 he was appointed Apostolic Administrator of the Diocese of Victoria. The Very Reverend A. J. Brabant died in 1912.

EDITED BY

Charles Lillard

MISSION TO
NOOTKA

1874-1900

*Reminiscences of the West Coast
of Vancouver Island*

Gray's Publishing Ltd.

SIDNEY, BRITISH COLUMBIA, CANADA

1977

Canadian Cataloguing in Publication Data

Brabant, Augustin Joseph, 1845-1912.
    Mission to Nootka, 1874-1900

        Bibliography: p. 119
        Includes index.
        ISBN 0-88826-072-5

        1. Brabant, Augustin Joseph, 1845-1912.
    2. Missionaries — Biography. 3. Missions —
    British Columbia — Vancouver Island. 4.
    Catholic Church — Missions. I. Lillard,
    Charles, 1944-   II. Title.

    BV2813.B73A3   266'.2'0924   C77-002119-0

47,660

ACKNOWLEDGEMENTS
Unless otherwise acknowledged the photographs in this book
were provided by the Provincial Archives of British Columbia.
I would like to take this opportunity to thank Howard Gerwing,
Chris Petter and Joan Ryan of the University of Victoria's
Special Collections for their assistance.

Designed and printed in Canada by
MORRISS PRINTING COMPANY LTD.
Victoria, British Columbia

Preface

This is the fourth time that Father Brabant's book has appeared in print. It was originally published as a serial in *The Messenger of the Sacred Heart*. In 1900 it appeared under the title *Vancouver Island and Its Missions*. Reverend Van Der Heyden used a great deal of the book in his *Life and Letters of Father Brabant* (1920) and the Reverend Moser incorporated it into his own *Reminiscences of the West Coast of Vancouver Island* in 1926. Then the world forgot *Vancouver Island and Its Missions*. It was forgotten for good reasons. Father Brabant's writing was atrocious, few of his statements corresponded to the known facts and the book was written for propaganda purposes.

Despite the book's defects, it is an important document. It stands alongside Father Morice's *History of the Northern Interior of British Columbia*, Reverend Collison's *In the Wake of the War Canoe*, Crosby's *An-ko-me-nums* and Bishop Ridley's *Snapshots from the North Pacific* as a record of a transitional period in British Columbian history. These books are eye-witness accounts of the collapse of various Indian cultures, and the authors were instrumental to the collapse. They had one aim in life: "to civilize the savages."

Father Brabant was a product of the 19th century. "Civilization," by his definition, was far more important than an age-old culture. He is a part of our history, as is this book. It is the record of one man's attempt to create order out of what he considered chaos. By no stretch of the imagination was the good Father a particularly observant man. But, while he never mentions totems or house poles, his descriptions of the Winter Ceremonial — the *Klookwana* — are as definitive as any in print. An apologist might defend many of the defects in this book, and there are many. He lacked Morice's scholarly curiosity, and he did not have Collison's sense of history. However, little will alter the major reason for reading Brabant. The Father was an average man working against super-human odds. The Nootkans kept slaves, practised shamanism and honoured their gods. In short they were living as they had for centuries; and almost single-handedly Father Brabant changed a civilization. How many men can say that?

5

Today we may not admire the results of Father Brabant's zeal, but we must, in the end, admire his courage and tenacity. He lived up to the demands of his Church. He ranks with Baranov, Judge Begbie and Father Duncan; all were Quixotes who forced their vision on the Pacific northwest.

Note to the text: If this book has had three lives, it has also had three faces. The author altered the text for book publication, and Father Moser added material when he used it to create his *Reminiscences*. Father Van Der Heyden used it, then confused the text with archival material — letters from Father Brabant to his relatives and superiors in Belgium. In this, its fourth life, it has been altered once again.

Since the text I have used, the 1900 edition, was written hurriedly for a coterie, I have cut all the overtly religious references except where they are a reflection of the author's state of mind. The text has been rearranged syntactically, and much of it has been rewritten for grammatical reasons. Due to his spelling and his use of variants, few of the author's place or tribal names could be located in dictionaries, gazetteers or on contemporary maps; the spelling of these has been modernized. Nothing has been added that was not in the original text.

Charles Lillard
Ross Bay
Vancouver Island

List of Illustrations

Augustin Joseph Brabant	FRONTISPIECE
Map	8
The Right Reverend Charles J. Seghers	14
Captain, officers and sailors of *H.M.S. Boxer*	26
Clayoquot beach camp	35
Hesquiat Church	37
A group of Indians with their chief, Matlahaw	40
Frederick Thornberg, his daughter and two sons	44
Hesquiat Mission	47
Reverend Father Brabant, ca. 1877	51
Grave monument of Chief Mokwinna	81
Sealing schooners in Victoria Harbour, ca. 1880	92
Captain E. Harlow, Mrs. A. Harlow and their two boys	96
"Manosaht" Indians and sailors	99
H.M.S. Boxer at anchor, Friendly Cove	101
Clayoquot Village, Stubbs Island	104
Harry Guillod, Indian Agent	105
Friendly Cove Village	108
Nootka Mission	110
Father Brabant's dream — Christie Indian School	115

THE FIELD OF LABOUR

On the west coast of Vancouver Island, between the entrance of the Strait of Juan de Fuca and Cape Cook, there live eighteen different tribes of Indians, forming, as it were, only one nation, as they all speak the same language.[1] Their manners, mode of living and all their habits are so much alike, that to know one tribe is to know them all. This coast, at the time of our taking possession of it, was exclusively inhabited by Indians.

Four trading posts had, however, been established and were each in charge of one white man. But besides these four men there were absolutely no white settlers to be found on this extensive coast of nearly two hundred miles.

I need hardly say that communication was very rare. Beyond a couple of small schooners that made an occasional call of the coast for the purpose of supplying the stores with goods and provisions, and at the same time making a trading call at different tribes, no vessels frequented this part of the world. I have been as much as six months without seeing the face of a white man and consequently speaking a civilized language.

When the news of the death of Pius IX reached me, Leo XIII was already two months on the Papal throne. As a matter of fact, it was close on five months since I had received a newspaper, a letter or a word of news of the civilized world.

All the Indians of this mission live on the sea coast, and intercourse between the tribes is impossible, except by means of canoes. No two tribes can visit each other, either on foot or horseback, as their several residences are separated by inlets and arms of the ocean. As a rule the number of chances for visiting are limited, especially during the fall and winter season, for no canoe could live in the incessant heavy weather and indescribable gales which rage on this open coast. When travelling I have been many a time compelled to camp and wait for days before being able to continue my journey, owing to the dangerous seas and heavy surf which would spring up without even an hour's notice.

The coast is rugged and rocky, presenting in its entire extent the appearance of desolation and barrenness.[2] The hills and mountains run down to the beach; the valleys are lakes, and a few patches of low land, to be encountered here and there, are covered with worthless timber. No clear land is to be seen anywhere, and no hopes can be entertained that the west coast of Vancouver Island will ever be available for agricultural settlements.

The climate is not very often different from that of Victoria. The seasons of rain and fine weather are about equally divided; the frost is not heavy, the snow seldom falls to any depth, and then lies on the ground only for a few days. With all this, the fall and winter months are dreary beyond expression. The Indians seem not to notice the general depression of the seasons. For one born and raised elsewhere, accustomed to the society of his fellow white men, there are no words to convey how monotonous it is, and how lonesome one would feel were it not for the thought of the sacredness of the object for which he is here.

Nothing in the world could tempt me to come and spend my life here were it not that the inhabitants of these inhospitable shores have a claim on the charity and zeal of a Catholic priest.

The question has often been asked: Was there ever a Catholic priest or were there Catholic missions established on the west coast before the existence of the present establishments?

My answer, which is in the affirmative, was not sought or found in books or records. I got it from the Indians themselves. My first informant was an elderly man, one of those men of importance to be found in every tribe, whose chief pride seems to consist in watching all the important events of the day and assisting the chiefs with the counsel and judgement.

I found my informant, Kragsota, on an early summer morning sitting outside of his house in close conversation with his wife. As I passed by he hailed me and our conversation commenced.

"Was there ever a priest in Nootka?"

"Oh yes," he said, "at the time of the Spaniards there were two priests, big stout men, and they both were bald-headed. My grand-uncle, who told me this, used to come around to Friendly Cove, and the white men would keep Sunday. There was the Sunday-house" — pointing to a spot about the centre of the present village — "and they would go on their knees and cross themselves. At the turn of the winter solstice they had a great Sunday and they had two babies — is not that what you now call Christmas? Oh yes, there were priests here, and all the men and women would have to bath on Saturday and be ready for Sunday. They learned songs — hymns — I know them yet."

10

And the old man began to sing, but the only words I could catch were: *Mi-Dios*.

It is evident from the above narrative that at the time of the occupation of Nootka by the Spaniards, towards the end of the last century, their missionaries belonged to the Franciscan order. Hence they are described by the Indian as being bald, on account of the tonsure and as stout, big men, because of their heavy Franciscan cloaks.

The old man had much more to say about the presence of the Spaniards in Nootka. One of the men was in charge of the cattle, which he would bring home every day. He also showed us the spot where the blacksmiths and carpenters had their shops, and gave many other details, which proves that events of importance are not so soon forgotten by Indians, in general, as white men unacquainted with them would imagine.[3]

I have not noticed any traces of religious practices inaugurated by Catholic Spaniards. However, it has struck me as probable that the great devotion of the Spaniards to the Blessed Virgin Mary and especially that of Catholic sailors, may have been the source of an invocation frequently uttered by Indians during bad weather or in danger at sea. Many a time I have heard them sing out in quick succession: "Chou-chist Hakoom, Chou-chist Hakoom," "Queen, let the sea be quiet." And many a time I have heard them speak of a "queen" unknown to them, but living in or beyond the seas.

I have also been inclined to believe that the practice of keeping Christmas and having the Christmas holidays may account for the Indians' yet having recourse at that special time to their devotional practices. It used to be of the greatest importance to watch and observe the solstice of the sun about Christmas time.[4] The old men of the tribe would rise early on those days and in bunches would retire to different spots. Each one had his mark or signs — there he would sit, all attention. As soon as the sun rose out of the sea, he would take his bearings.

If the sun rose at or beyond such a certain mark he would conclude that the sun was at its solstice, not yet at it, or perhaps beyond it.

The event caused an amount of general interest. It was the talk at meals and the great topic of conversation with the Indians of every tribe. According to the old men the want of attention, or the neglect of watching this all-important event, would be followed by all kinds of misfortunes, not excluding famine. The arrival of this period was the signal for the preaching of the old people to their young men to go out and practise their superstitious devotions.

Beyond these indifferent signs of religious practices which may have had their origin at the time of the settlement by the Spaniards at Nootka, I have never been able to detect anything. The Indians at the time of our arrival here were addicted beyond redemption to every description of pagan practices.

MISSIONS ESTABLISHED. VISIT TO THE WEST COAST INDIANS IN 1874 BY RIGHT REVEREND CHARLES SEGHERS, D.D., ACCOMPANIED BY REVEREND A.J. BRABANT

We left Victoria on Whitsunday at 8 in the morning on the schooner *Surprise*, twenty-eight tons, belonging to Captain W. Spring & Co.[5]

Captain Peter Francis was in command. John Peterson, a Swede, was Mate. The rest of the crew was a Kyuquot Indian called Nomucos, acting as cook, sailor and boatswain, and Chegchiepe, a Moachat savage, assistant sailor. Mr. John McDowell was a passenger, and was on his way to fix the machinery of the lighthouse just then established on Cape Beale, Barkley Sound.[6]

We left Victoria Harbour with a strong southeasterly wind, and were at Race Rocks before 10 o'clock a.m. Here the wind failed and our schooner began to drift about and working with the oars was required to keep her off the Rocks. However, we got safely at anchor about 2 in Becher Bay, where we went on shore and visited the Indians, from whom we received a good reception. After an address, made by his Lordship, I baptized two of their infant children.

April 13. — Next morning we weighed anchor. Sailed out a short distance, but the wind failed us again. We managed to return to our anchorage to make a new start about 8 a.m. Once more the breeze dropped and by this time we began to drift with the tide until we got half way between Race Rocks and Port Angeles. Our Captain was now so badly intoxicated that upon his Lordship's asking him the direction of Cape Flattery, with a view to trying the old man, he pointed to us the opening between San Juan Island and Trial Island. 2 p.m., southerly wind; lost sight of Victoria at 3:30.

April 14.—Rain; no wind; 7:30 a.m., southwest by south. Entered Port San Juan at 3:30 p.m. Cast anchor outside the reef at 3:30.

The schooner *Favorite*, Captain McKay, and the schooner *Alert*, Captain J. Christianson, were here at anchor, and were making preparations to go out sealing next morning with a crew of Nitinat and Pacheenaht Indians.

April 15. — We went on shore about 7 a.m. The Indians were sitting outside. They were startled to see us in our cassocks, to them an unusual kind of garment. The Bishop asked to see their chief and was soon shown into the presence of a fine looking man — Kwistog — who, as we noticed, at once, was then leading the life of a bigamist. His Lordship asked the Chief's consent to assemble the natives of that locality and he at once consented. Here I was suddenly compelled to make room for a blind horse, which was led into the house by a young Indian, and was then stabled in the Chief's house.

The Indians behaved very well and, upon allowing us to baptize their children, requested as a favour that we continue to look after them. The number of baptisms was forty-three.

The Captains of the sealing vessels were most impatient to take the Indians out. They were told that if the priests wanted the Indians to stay on shore three days they should have the privilege; which news was to them a caution to keep their temper. However, we left the Indians at 2 p.m.; we went on board of the *Surprise*; they in their turn went on board of their respective vessels.

The wind was blowing from the west and blew up into Port San Juan. The vessels weighed their anchors about the same time, had up sails and were readying for a start in unusually quick time. And now the race began. Our skipper was about sober and did his best to win, but the *Favorite* got ahead of him and before long the *Alert* went first and kept

The Right Reverend Charles J. Seghers,
Bishop of Victoria, ca. 1874.

14

ahead of her friends. The race was fairly conducted and was a very pleasant episode of our western trip.

April 16. — No wind. Caught a breeze at 12. Entered Dodger Channel at 1 p.m. The Chief was living alone on Diana Island. Two canoes full of Indians came over from Keeshan,[7] but were told to go back till next morning, which they did with considerable reluctance. The Indians looked well, a fine, healthy set. They wore blankets, no pants, and had their hair nicely done up and tied with grass in a bunch over the forehead. Most of them had their faces painted, and the crowd that came on the schooner presented a very picturesque sight.

April 17. — Said Mass in the house of Mr. Andrew Lang,[8] the storekeeper, at 5 a.m. The Chief was already there addressing his Indians from the other side of the stream, exhorting them to rise, wash and clean themselves and their children, announcing to them our wish to see them and telling them that great things were in store for them.

The Indians arrived from Keeshan and other camping places and assembled at 8 in the house of an Indian called "Jenkins," the Chief having no house large enough at this place to contain all his people. The savages paid great attention to the Bishop's instruction given in Chinook and interpreted into the Indian language by "Harry" and his brother "Jenkins."

In this and in every tribe on the coast instruction was begun by stating who we were, what was our object; then followed a history of the creation, the fall of man, the deluge, the multiplication of languages, the redemption of mankind. After which, if agreeable to the natives, baptism was administered to their little children. And, if time was left, a few hymns and songs were taught. But in all cases the teaching of the Sign of the Cross and the making of that sign by the Indians was the great thing and caused real excitement. We had in this camp eighty baptisms of young children.

We left at 6 o'clock in the evening and went to our anchor at Clarkkonikose, Effingham Island, Barkley Sound, where we passed a very comfortable night in smooth water.

April 18. — Up and away at 5 a.m. Rain, heavy sea. We arrived at 9 a.m. at Ucluelet, where the Indians were expecting us. The Chief came at once for us in his canoe. Upon nearing the camp one of the Indians fired off his gun to announce to the Indians that we were on board, whereupon all the tribe turned out at once and assembled in the new, unfinished house of young Wish Koutl, the Chief of the Ucluelets. Our arrival caused a great deal of excitement. Our interpreter had a thundering voice, but we were told he did not translate His Lordship's words with much correctness.[9] Perhaps he thought that shouting would have the necessary effect. I baptized seventy-five children in the afternoon.

April 19. — Sunday morning: Mass at 5:30 in the storekeeper's house and then at 8 a.m. off to the rancherie.[10] The Clayoquot Indians came over to join the Ucluelets and their nine children received baptism. Here the first effort was made to translate the sign of the Cross into the Indian language.

April 20. — At sunrise we were already at sea and beating against a strong westerly wind, but we did not reach Clayoquot till April 21, at 9 a.m. Sitakenin and half a dozen of his Indians came out to meet us at sea. We went on board of his canoe and he took us to the Chief's house. There two new Indian mats were laid on the floor, forming a path to the end of the lodge, where boxes and trunks covered with fine mats were prepared to be used by us as seats and footstools. His Lordship addressed the Indians on the usual topics; then I baptized ninety-three children, after which we returned to our schooner, which was at anchor off Seddall Island, Warren's store.

April 22. — We went early in the morning to Ehchachist, Effingham Island, where we met the Indians of the day before. Strange to say, the Indians seemed quite indifferent and His Lordship concluded to leave them, not, however, before giving them a good scolding. Then we went to the schooner about noon and preparations were at once made to continue our voyage. After sailing a short distance we got on the sand bank off Opitsat, but as the tide was rising, we got off about 1:30 p.m. Then with a light breeze we took the direction of Ahousat, but about 3 p.m. we saw a canoe in the distance. The Clayoquot Chief and six young men! They wanted us to return. The Bishop at first refused, but their request was so earnest and their promise of taking us to Ahousat the next day so favourable, that His Lordship at last concluded to return. The Indians who came to fetch us had only just then arrived in the schooner from Ucluelet, where they had seen us for a few minutes two days previously. They had tried to meet us at their own home. They were doubly disappointed to find us gone and to hear that their friends had not shown more zeal and had failed to learn the canticles and songs now repeated by every tribe which we had visited.

At 6 p.m. we were at work again at Ehchachist and we were happy that at 10:30 p.m. the Indians at last allowed us to lie down and take some rest. This was my first night in an Indian camp and in the morning my memory was clear on all the events of that night. I had heard the crying of Indian children, and the coaxing and singing of their mothers to get them to sleep again. An old couple had a row in the middle of the night. Over a dozen big dogs growled, barked, fought and yelled, ran in and out of the dwelling and got in trouble with the cats. They would not stop their uproar, except after twenty "Tsiekas" [11] uttered by a sleepless savage, followed by a piece of firewood, again accompanied by a new yelling and barking. Over half a dozen roosters were sleeping on the loft cross-piece of the house. With their usual pride, as if they were making daylight come and the sun rise, they would stop their crowing chorus, only to recommence again a few minutes later. All this time the Bishop thought I was fast asleep alongside of him under one blanket. But I knew that he was not, for he was continually turning about. Now and then he would give a quick but well determined scratch on his lower limbs. In the morning he told me that all the cause of his troubles had been the Indians' friends, the fleas.

April 23. — At 5:30 our Indian crew was ready; six stalwart young men, headed by the chief of the tribe. It was a beautiful morning, the sun rising in all his glory. The Indians struck up our songs and paddled with courage and happiness over the calm waters of Clayoquot Sound.

At 1 o'clock we arrived at the foot of the Catface Mountains. Here was the Ahousaht tribe, in expectation of our coming, increased by the arrival of all the Kelsemahts, ready and prepared to receive us. Four Indians stood on the beach, and were a deputation sent by the Indians, who were already in the Chief's house, to show us into the lodge. Mats formed a pathway from the water to the camp and, inside, mats and sails were hanging about along the walls. The floor was covered with more mats, and a regular throne was formed, with boxes and trunks, nicely covered over; and to this place we were shown by the members of the deputation. A dead silence reigned in the house, but we could well notice that we were in the presence of real savages. We were astonished that no dogs, such a nuisance about Indian camps, were to be noticed. We were next informed that, already the day previous and early in the morning, canoe loads of the canine species had been taken across the Sound and safely landed on the islands opposite, lest they should be a cause of displeasure to us.

In the evening we were requested to listen to what they had to say to us. The speeches began by those of the two head chiefs, followed by other chiefs, chiefly women. One fellow got up, took his blanket, his only covering, from his shoulders, and after showing it to us, he threw it with an emphatic gesture far away from him, saying that "he threw away his bad heart." Nothing could stop the speech-making until His

17

Lordship stepped forward on the very spot where every speaker had come to address us, and thus blocked the way.

We left the Ahousahts April 24, at 4:30 a.m. A good easterly wind was blowing, and the Captain concluded to run for Kyuquot and call at the other tribes on our way back. So we did, and arrived at the Kyuquot camp shortly after 3 p.m.

Here not an Indian could be seen on the bay, nor, in fact, outside of the camp. It was pronounced an unusual thing, as the captain stated that these Indians used to meet him out at sea and literally crowd the deck of his schooner on any other occasion. Nomucos, our Kyuquot cook, was also at a loss to explain, and his shouting and calling for the Indians had no effect. However, at last a small canoe was launched at Aktese, two Indians got into her and paddled quickly to the spot where we were at anchor. Every little while they would stop and listen to the shouting of our Indians. "We are afraid," was the first sentence we could hear them utter. Our savages reassured them and when at last they got on board they explained the whole mystery. They had heard of our arrival, but the story got mixed up. On board the schooner was a living man who would cut the children on the chest, and another who would rub something over the wound and it would be healed. Then the first man would begin killing the Indians, and upon the Indians' trying to kill him, he would turn into a stone or become a stone man. This and other tales were told as an explanation of the conduct of the Kyoquots on this occasion. The Kyoquots are the largest tribe on the coast, in all about eight hundred Indians.

April 26. — Baptized one hundred and seventy-seven children. I commenced at 9 o'clock in the morning and it was 5 o'clock in the afternoon when I got through.

April 27. — Frightful storm at sea — could not go on shore all day.

April 28. — At 1 p.m. we were taken from the *Surprise* in an Indian canoe, as we had made arrangement to go with some of Kyuquot Indians and visit the Checkleset tribe.

The Chief, a cripple, seemed to have great authority, but being himself unable to go with us, he sent his son with fifteen young men to take us to our destination. No sooner had we stepped into our canoe than two more canoes were put afloat. The first was manned by fifteen young men, the subjects of the queen, and the other by twelve savages belonging to the other head chiefs. And thus we left Kyoquot in the young chief's canoe, on either side of which a canoe of the other chiefs was paddled to the air of one of the hymns they had recently learned.

The sea was very rough, but after three hours of hard working by the

Indians we at last saw the smoke of the Checkleset camp at Acous. As we approached our Indians drew together and once more intoned some of our Catholic hymns. The Checklesets came rushing out of their houses, and seemed quite stupefied, but did not come down to the beach till they were called upon to do so. It took them a long time to assemble in the Chief's house, and when addressed by His Lordship, although seemingly attentive, it was quite evident that everything was not "all right." The evening and darkness soon put a stop to our work; then we began to look for room to sleep. It was simply horrible! The filth, dirt and uncleanness of these Indians both in the house and outside cannot be imagined. However, we submitted to circumstances, such as they were, and lay down alongside of each other, impatiently awaiting the return of daylight. It arrived at last. I was amused when asked by His Lordship to express my opinion of the beauty of the words and music which he had composed during the night. It struck me that, unable to sleep, he must have tried to while away the long hours of a sleepless night in a musical way. The Kyuquots, forty-three in number, who had constituted our escort, having noticed that there was something wrong in our reception extended to us by the Checklesets, had made it a point of duty to sleep in the same house where we were sleeping. In the morning we found them lying around us.

April 29. — Early in the morning we assembled the Indians and began anew to instruct them. When this was done, our Kyuquot interpreter refused to interpret, and gave for his reason that the Checklesets were mocking and insulting him. We would have left at once, but the sea was bad and the rain fell in torrents. Being compelled to stay, we began the recitation of our office and went outside in the bush under the shelter of a large tree. Here, after some time, an Indian found us enjoying the fresh air and summoned us to go back to the camp. We pretended not to understand, but at last His Lordship concluded to follow the savage and so we re-entered the Chief's lodge. It was quite a sight. To the western side of the camp sat the Chief in a very prominent place, and on each side sat an elderly man holding in his hand a long rod, which seemed to us to be a mark of authority. Everything was still, the men on our side, the women and children on the other. A seat was shown to us on the right side of the Chief, where we were requested to continue our instructions. But none of the young men could interpret and not one of our Kyuquots was about, nor, in fact, could be gotten.

This seemed very strange, but the following explanation was afterward given. For years the Checklesets and the Kyuquots had been at

19

war or giving annoyance to each other. The Checklesets on this occasion did not relish the presence of the Kyuquots. One of them had invited them to go and eat in his house to get them out of the way. Then he had quickly locked up the house, and when the Kyuquots wanted to go and join us they found the entrance of the lodge locked up fast. Great was their indignation when at last they came back in our presence. Angry words, speeches and gesticulations were the order of the hour.

April 30. — We left the Checklesets and arrived in Kyuquot in due time. On May 1, we had the happiness of offering up the holy sacrifice of the Mass in honour of the Blessed Virgin Mary, putting our new mission under her special protection.

His Lordship having noticed the good dispositions of the Kyuquots had, before going to Checkleset, asked the Captain of the *Surprise* to make a large mission cross, which we found ready upon our arrival. The cross was twenty-four feet long, with the cross-piece in proportion. It was the work of not only the Captain, but Peterson, the Mate, a Swedish Lutheran.

Before proceeding to plant it, we were called to the house of the Chief, where we found all the men of the tribe assembled. After asking our permission, they began to sing some of their savage songs with great solemnity. Then they showed us a mask, the handiwork of northern Indians, most ingeniously made; also a piece of glass to which they seemed to attach unusual importance; as well as a number of beads held in great esteem by all the Indians on this coast. Beads are sold by one tribe to another at the most exorbitant prices. After a speech from His Lordship, condemning all Indian superstitions in general, several important men got up and promised to go by our instructions.

After this we proceeded to the blessing of the cross. It was placed on three canoes and about fifty young men took charge. An immense number of Indians followed us in canoes to the foot of a small island opposite the shore, then unoccupied and seemingly abandoned. And there it now stands in sight of the tribe. It was beautiful to see the Indians struggle to carry the heavy burden, preceded by His Lordship. When it was raised, fifty muskets were fired off as if to announce a great triumph to the savages on the Kyuquot islands.

We left on May 2, taking the direction of Quatsino Sound. However, the wind was contrary, and His Lordship came to the conclusion, after consulting the Captain, to abandon his trip to Quatsino Sound. Thus we sailed before the wind, and arrived that evening at an anchorage in Esperanza Inlet, before the camp of the Nuchatlaht Indians.

May 3. — Early this morning we were taken in a canoe, by the Chief of the Nuchatlahts and a crew of young men, to the outside camp, where the Indians were at this time living.

The reception given to us by the Nuchatlahts was something never to be forgotten. The news of our arrival had preceded us. The Chief had made a new house and a wharf about two hundred feet in length, but only about four feet in breadth, had been constructed. Although the Indians deserved credit for making such extraordinary preparations, we had to measure our steps and movements, lest the whole structure should break down. Inside the Chief's house the ground was covered with white sand. Our path and the room which we were to occupy were laid with new mats; the walls were hung with sails of canoes and pieces of calico. Twenty-nine sea otter skins, valued by Captain Francis, of the *Surprise*, at close to two thousand dollars, were hanging in a line opposite to where we were sitting, and excited our admiration.

The Ehattesaht Indians had come across and joined the Nuchatlahts. In the afternoon a disturbance between the two tribes took place. Our interpreter was of little account, and our success was not in keeping with the great preparations they had made to receive us. However, before we left, harmony had been restored. The Ehattesahts went home and we returned to the *Surprise*, where we remained until May 4.

At 1:15, a slight breeze sprang up, and we slowly sailed up Esperanza Inlet. By dark we were near the Nootka Straits, and we fastened the schooner with a rope to a tree alongside immense bluffs of perpendicular rocks, where we passed the night. Another night was passed before we got to the Nootka side, part of the day having been spent by the captain and his passengers fishing for rock cod.

May 6. — After pulling up the oars and dragging the schooner alongside of the rocks for a considerable time, we at last got through the Narrows. This morning we had a strong land breeze which took us to Bligh Island, then beat against the breeze from Muchalat Inlet, and later the westerly wind came to our assistance. We arrived at the Muchalat village of Cheeshish at half-past twelve p.m.

Here, also, great preparations had been made, and an Ahousaht Indian, Muggins by name, was there with Muchalat young men to take us on shore from the schooner. This Indian had profited by our instructions to his own tribe. Upon the request of the Muchalats he had taught them the Sign of the Cross and some of our hymns.

May 7. — was spent with the Indians. The Captain in the intervals of his trading, filled his schooner literally up with deer and elk skins.

May 8. — We started this morning at 4 with a northerly breeze and cast anchor at 10:30 a.m. in Friendly Cove.

Here we met a large tribe of Indians, very noisy and disorderly compared with other tribes. We understood the cause of the dispositions of the Indians to be the talk against the priests by Fort Rupert women who were living here,[12] and by a few Indians who had been slaves or had resided at the other side of the Island. However, we stayed another day and left May 10. After sailing before a westerly wind, we arrived in Hesquiat shortly before noon. Here we learned that the Indians expecting our coming had been afraid to go out fishing for several weeks. They had cleaned and laid mats in the Chief's house — they were very neatly dressed, the women all in white calico, the men having made pants and coats of blankets.

May 11. — We rose at an early hour and recommenced our instructions, but by this time the Captain was anxious to return to town as soon as possible. At 11 his sails went up as a sign that we were wanted on board. The Indians seemed very sorry and disappointed, but we left, promising to visit them again in the near future.

May 12. — When off Clayoquot Sound nine Kyuquot canoes, seventy-three men and one woman, overtook us. Our visit over the coast had taken away all fear. Only two or three of the crowd had ever been to Victoria and none in an Indian canoe; doing so would have exposed them to the danger of being killed or being made slaves by hostile tribes.

May 13. — We arrived in Dodger Channel. There was no wind and this gave us a chance to go and visit the Uchuklesaht Indians. The Chief was alongside of the schooner and took us to his camp, where he assembled the Indians. That evening he took us back to Dodger Channel where we arrived at 11 p.m. Everyone was in bed. We had no supper, as everybody seemed or pretended to sleep. We turned in with the happy thought that our work was over.

May 14. — We said Mass at the store-keeper's house at 5 a.m., then went on board and left the cove sometime before noon.

May 15. — We ran before a fine westerly wind and arrived in Victoria at 8 p.m.

SECOND VISIT TO THE WEST COAST INDIANS IN 1874 BY THE RIGHT REVEREND BISHOP SEGHERS, D.D., AND REVEREND A.J. BRABANT

The day of our departure was the first of September. Two days before, Captain Francis had been married in St. Andrew's Cathedral by Reverend Father Brabant to Cecilia, a half-breed girl, the niece of Mrs. Lequier. The effects of the feast were visible on the skipper's countenance and in his manners. As a first mishap, the man who was to act as Mate did not turn up at the hour agreed upon by the Captain. However, after a run on the shore by one of the boys, we saw him at last. Upon crawling on board he mentioned the cause of the delay was that his concubine, a Haida woman, had run away. This, our Mate, was a Greek, and also rejoiced in the name of Frank. Thus, with two Franks and two Indians from the coast, and, as we discovered afterwards, with plenty of whiskey on board, we started on our second visit to our West Coast Indians.

The first few hours were spent pleasantly, but when we got to the Straits, our skipper began to make frequent calls down in the cabin. At last we discovered that he was getting very drunk. This rather alarmed us, as Frank, our Greek Mate, had never been on the coast and our sailors could not be relied upon. His Lordship advised me to try and find out where the Captain kept his liquor and throw it overboard.

Meanwhile, Frank, the Greek, came down and told us that he had taken charge of and hidden all the liquor on board. It was now great fun to watch the skipper. He went downstairs on his old errand. He pretended to whistle so as to be unnoticed, then he looked up at the staircase, then made for the locker, but nothing there! Where could the liquor be? He did not say a word about it. Meanwhile he silently cursed at his clerical passengers and told the Mate of it; then he begged him for a little drink. It was refused at first; later on, something was given him now and then to sober him up. All this time the old man was growling at us and blaming us for taking his favourite beverage, never suspecting for a moment that the liquor which was given to sober him up was his own property.

Although the measure adopted had the effect of keeping the old man from greater excess, still he was far from being sober when we entered

Pachena Bay. The wind was blowing fresh from the west when we entered the harbour. Our schooner was supposed to go up the river to discharge at the store kept by Neils Moos. We were going full speed when she suddenly struck a sand bar. The channel had shifted, or rather our Captain was out of his reckonings through whiskey! Every wave took her higher and higher, but Neils Moos came on board and saved her from ruin. We took charge without heeding our drunken captain, and an hour later she was at anchor before Captain Spring & Co.'s store.

Nothing of much consequence occurred, but when we left for Barkley Sound we met at the mouth of San Juan Harbour a canoe from Victoria with a supply of whiskey. By and by we saw the H.M.S. *Boxer* come out of Neah Bay and steam for the Pachena village. Dr. Powell, Superintendent of Indian Affairs, was on board, and this was his first trip along the coast. When he landed at the rancherie he found every man, save the Chief, beastly drunk.

We got in Barkley Sound on the 7th of September. The Ohiet Indians had moved up the Sound and after discharging freight at the store in Dodger Channel we continued our journey to Ucluelet.

Here the schooner *Surprise* was to stop and we were to continue on our trip in our Indian canoe. Consequently Captain Francis gave us as pilots two Kyuquot Indians, who had been engaged as deckhands on the *Surprise* and also a good sealing canoe, besides lots of provisions.

We bade him and his young wife goodbye and a happy honeymoon on the 8th of September, at 7 o'clock. And now we were on the open ocean in a small sealing canoe with two Kyuquot and one Ehattesaht Indians.

The sea was heavy and no wind. An occasional wave broke over our bows and did considerable damage to our stock of provisions, especially to our biscuits and sack of flour.

Without further mishap we arrived at Opitsat, Clayoquot Sound, at about 2 p.m. The Indians were very much excited over the news that a man-of-war was anchored to the leeward of Vargas Island with the Superintendent of Indian Affairs on board. We continued our voyage and about 4 o'clock we saw the H.M.S. *Boxer* at anchor at the above-named place. All this time we had not a breath of wind. Our Indians kept on paddling and we went at last on shore on Flores Island, just opposite one of the Ahousaht villages called Seektukis.

It was not a good camping place, and the hour being rather late and the night dark, we felt compelled to stretch our weary limbs without even taking a warm drink of tea. We were enjoying our sleep as best as we could when all of a sudden, sometime after midnight, an Ahousaht Indian came to wake us up. He was sent by the tribe. They were all up and expected us to go over. But His Lordship prevailed upon him to let us enjoy our camping out rather than go two miles across the Sound in the middle of the night and avail ourselves of the Indians' hospitality. When at last the Indian concluded to leave us, he went away saying that we were very lazy.

Shortly after our Ahousaht visitor had left us, we were again aroused from our slumber by the noise of some Hesquiat Indians, who were on their way to Ahousat. They wanted to know who we were, where we came from and where we were going, and finished by saying that the sea was very rough on the outside. When we awoke next morning, we made a large fire. At daylight we could see that we had camped in a very poor place, as it began to rain, which prevented us from leaving; we had occasion to spend some very dreary hours on that spot. At noon the weather cleared up and then we proceeded on our voyage till we arrived, about 5 p.m., at Hot Springs Cove.

Here quite a number of Hesquiat Indians were living, and as the man-of-war was now anchored in the Cove and had been followed by a large number of Ahousahts and some Clayoquots, the place presented quite a lively appearance. A number of junior officers and blue-jackets were on shore. When we had just pitched our tent we received the visit of Mr. Tim Scanlan, an Irishman, who acted as Steward on board the vessel. He told us, in a rich Irish brogue, wherein we were wrong to be travelling at such a time of year and in such a canoe. He added that the Captain of the vessel had repeatedly spoken of us and was determined to pick us up whenever he would meet us. At the request of His Lordship, Mr. Scanlan promised not to make the Captain aware of our presence. Soon Tim came back with a supply of provisions in the shape of some loaves of fresh bread, a leg of mutton, a quarter of elk, two bottles of wine and one bottle of brandy. Upon his suggestion, we opened the bottle of wine and drank to the health of His Lordship, the Bishop, who in his turn proposed the health of Tim Scanlan. This scene was without outside witnesses, and took place on the evening of the 9th of September, 1874, in Hot Springs Cove.

Next morning we were having our breakfast when the man-of-war steamed out of Hot Springs Cove and we resumed our journey as soon as that transaction was over. No wind, a heavy sea and the sun burning over our heads made the crossing of Hesquiat Harbour anything but pleasant. Besides, our Indians had indigestion and were all three very seasick. One of them, between intervals of vomiting, would carelessly sing old Indian songs. This afforded us, if not recreation, at least a topic to speak about. At noon we took dinner in front of the Hesquiat outside camp, Homais. Then we went on shore again on the Escalante Rocks, whence we paddled to Friendly Cove, Nootka Sound.

There, to our horror, we again found the *Boxer* at anchor. While we were boiling our cup of tea and the Indians were putting up our tent we received once more the visit of our friend of yesterday, Mr. Tim Scanlan, who brought us another bottle of brandy. At the same time he announced that the Captain had ordered his boat to be lowered and that with the Superintendent he would come on shore and invite us to go on board his vessel. And indeed before we had taken our tea, we were introduced to Captain Collins, of the Royal Navy, and by him prevailed upon to abandon our way of travelling and avail ourselves of the accommodation of an English man-of-war to continue our journey.

The Captain, we understood, was a staunch member of the Anglican Church, and every day held divine service on board. He kept a

Captain, officers and sailors of *H.M.S. Boxer* at Nootka Sound.

bank for the men and had established a temperance society for them. He made our stay on board most enjoyable and, as it happened to be on a Friday, he kindly and delicately had matters arranged in such a way that the abstinence enjoyed by the Church on that day was easily observed.

The weather was thick and foggy, but we managed to pass the Nootka Narrows long before noon. We went as far as Catala Island and anchored there for a time. As it was not allowed by the rules of the navy to go out in the foggy, uncertain weather, the Captain concluded to run for Queen's Cove and there spend the night at anchor in smooth water. A beautiful hammock was fixed up as a bed for His Lordship, the Bishop, and a bed was prepared for me on a sofa. Our Indians were made comfortable below with the Marines. We left next morning at 5, got as far as Catala Island, but owing to the state of the weather and sea we once more returned to Queen's Cove. At noon we made a fresh start and running as we did before a fresh easterly breeze, we arrived early in the afternoon to anchor in Man-of-War Harbour, Kyuquot Sound.

We left H.M.S. *Boxer* next morning at 5. Our canoe, which had been taken on board at Friendly Cove, was lowered. The liberality of Tim Scanlan, under orders of the Captain, has so much increased our stock of provisions that by the time we got in her, we were deeply loaded. It was impossible or dangerous to look behind us to cast a last look on the fine war vessel, on which we had spent two most enjoyable days.

And now we were on shore in Kyuquot Sound! We took up our headquarters in Captain Spring's old and unoccupied store. We went to Chickluat next day, where we did very little besides baptizing one child. We soon discovered that we had chosen a bad time of year to find the Kyuquots. They were camped at a dozen different places, but His Lordship concluded that he would go and see the Chief. He was at the end of Bokshis Inlet and there we met him next day with a few more Indians. We baptized a few newly-born children. His Lordship prepared a young girl who was at the point of death, but nothing else could be accomplished. His Lordship had bought from the Chief, for a few biscuits, a wood bucket representing an animal. The tail was the handle, the body the body of the bucket, and the head and mouth the passages through which the water or liquid was poured. It was a curious piece of work and very artistically done. Together with some masks got also at this place, it was given, as a souvenir of our trip, to Captain Collins of H.M.S. *Boxer*. He felt so proud of the gift that he afterwards exhibited it in one of the principal hotels in Victoria.

September 17. — The Chief sent his son and six other young men next day to where we expressed the wish to go, namely the Nuchatlaht village. We had a quick but rough passage; at one time the sea struck our canoe and nearly filled her up with water.

At Nuchatlaht we did very little or no good. The disposition of the Indians being very indifferent, it cost us quite an amount of trouble to get the crew to take us to the next tribe. Finally three old men volunteered, and that night we were amongst the Nootkas camped at Tahsis. We found these Indians in full glee — a dead whale had drifted on their land and the houses were full of blubber, which the women were boiling and reducing to oil. I do not think that anything that we could have said under the circumstances would have had much effect, as the whale was uppermost in their minds.

We stayed only one night at Nuchatlaht. Then, with a small crew, we went down the Sound. At Etawinni we baptized a few children. Since we could not get to Muchalat that day, we slept at a place called Ois. The next morning we went to Hoiss, where the Muchalat Chief was camped.

As we went on shore at Ois the evening before, a Muchalat canoe had seen us and reported our approach to their friends. The tribe at once appeared to receive us. Messengers had been sent the very night to all fishing stations, and by the time we arrived we learned that the tribe was collecting on the other side of the Sound.

September 21. — At 11 as a strong westerly wind was blowing up Muchalat Inlet, ten canoes filled with Indians put up sail on the other side and steered for Hoiss. It was a sight never to be forgotten: the enthusiasm of these Indians and the taste displayed in their arrangements for our reception. They were all nicely dressed, the women in white calico robes and the men with pants and coats. We assembled them at once and stayed with them for three days. Most of the Indians were living under tents made with their canoe sails, at all times a poor shelter, but especially at this season of the year. But upon expressing our feelings of sorrow for them, as it was raining most of the time, they pleasantly replied that the rain did not cause them any inconvenience. They insisted we should not leave them before they knew everything we had a mind to teach them. Such fervor and zeal we had not met in any other tribe and therefore, in order to encourage and reward them, His Lordship concluded to plant, at their principal camping place, another cross. This was done with great success, and in the same order as we had observed on the occasion of our first trip to Kyuquot.

September 25. — Next morning we left Muchalat in one of their canoes, with the chief and eleven of his young men, en route for Hesquiat. When off Perez Rock we met a Hesquiat canoe crowded with young men, who were on the lookout for our expected arrival. As soon as they recognized us, they put about, intending to precede us and warn the tribe. However, our Muchalat crew took to their paddles, and a regular race between the two canoes took place. There was no wind, and the sea ran mountains high. We had not met such a heavy swell in all our travels. Although in company with the Hesquiats, we would lose sight of them for several minutes to see them again rise on the crest of the heavy waves, whilst we were, as it were, in the abyss of the ocean. It was really a grand piece of sailing we had on that day from Perez Rock to Hesquiat Harbour. We at last lost sight of the Hesquiats in the fog, but we could hear them fire off their guns ahead of us as a signal to the tribe to be ready. We found the Chief's house, where we stayed for four days, cleanly swept out, and mats laid all over the floor. The Indians were full of joy to see us again.

We began our work at once; taught the Lord's Prayer, Hail Mary, Creed, Ten Commandments and Seven Sacraments, all of which the Indians learned with much zeal. Here it struck the Bishop that this tribe would be a good place to start a Mission, being the most central and the Indians of the best good-will. He mentioned the matter to the Chief, asking him to assemble the other Chiefs of the tribe and propose to them the matter in question. This having been done, we were informed, in the presence of the whole tribe, that land would be given for Mission buildings and other purposes and that we could have our choice as to locality. At the same time a spot was mentioned on the hill — according to the Bishop not desirable, being too much exposed to the northerly wind. As to the objection that the spot was surrounded by Indian houses, the Indians were willing to evacuate the village site and grant it for Mission purposes. During our stay at Hesquiat, as well as at Muchalat, we said Mass every morning at 5, at which all the Indians were present, and during which they recited the Holy Rosary. We here noticed every morning — and, in fact, whenever we assembled the Indians — such zeal and fervor that old men unable to walk were carried on the backs of the young men to the Chief's house, and some of them came on hands and feet.

The old Chief of Hesquiat, his son being absent at Cape Flattery, took us to Ahousat with a large crew of young men. We arrived in due time at Seektukis, the residence of Shiyous, the second Chief of the tribe. Maquinna, the first Chief, was sent for, but refused to come, having only lately lost one of his children. Shiyous at once sent several canoes to fetch the Indians from their different salmon rivers. The messengers travelled all night, and next morning quite a large number arrived and listened to the Bishop's instructions. But being over anxious to return to their homes that evening, a disturbance took place, and they got a severe reprimand from the Bishop. Afterwards things were settled, and the Indians left us in good humour, while we prepared to leave next morning.

October 1. — Shiyous and his oldest son and one of his slaves took us to Clayoquot. We found the Chief absent, but we were taken to the lodge of Sitakenin, where we slept.

October 2. — The Chief arrived next morning. We went over to see him, but as he was eating, His Lordship, the Bishop of Vancouver Island, and one of his priests were told to go outside. The Chief of the Clayoquots could not transact any business with them till he had finished eating his breakfast! After walking outside quite a time the Clayoquot Chief came to meet us. He asked our business and proposed to assemble the Indians there present in his house, which was not quite made up for the winter season. The Bishop spoke to them for some little time, after which I baptized four young children.

Having proposed to the Clayoquot Chief to take us to Ucluelet, he wished us to go with him up the Clayoquot Arm to his salmon station; he would from there cross to Wickaninnish Bay or Schooner Cove. If no canoe was at any of the outside camps it would be an easy task to pull a canoe across and put her afloat with our baggage at Wickaninnish Bay, which was, comparatively speaking, a short distance from Ucluelet Harbour. We complied with his desire, which gave us a chance to see Clayoquot Inlet. The entrance to the lake, and the muddy flats were literally alive with ducks and geese. The dreary hours that we spent at the Chief's house are painful to remember. The smoke and stench inside cannot be imagined. Besides, the house was so low and the abundance of salmon so great that we could not move except in a stooping position. And we could not put down a foot except on or over dissected salmon or salmon roe!

Therefore, we went outside and pitched our tent, and next morning we begged of the Chief as a favour to take us to Long Bay and thence to Ucluelet. The poor man seemed anxious to comply with our request, but upon coming to the seacoast he found that the surf would not allow launching a canoe. We were compelled to pitch our tent and await better weather. Meanwhile he went to his house and family, promising to come next day. He kept his word, but made the same remark as the day before — an easterly wind. Off he went again with the promise of another visit next day. Again he kept his word, but again the same difficulty — an easterly wind. This morning, upon rising, we noticed that our tent had been visited by a bear. His tracks were there, but finding the tent occupied, he had preferred to walk off rather than disturb us.

About noon His Lordship proposed to walk over the Indian trail to Ucluelet. The Clayoquots hardly approved of the idea, but promised to take our baggage to Captain Francis' house as soon as the weather would permit. With this promise the Bishop was satisfied and then ordered me to prepare some provisions, which I did with reluctance. Off we went, on foot, accompanied by two Kyuquot Indians who helped us in carrying the things that we had judged necessary to take along. We walked all that afternoon, first over a beautiful sandy beach; then we crossed a point and arrived in Florencia Bay, around which we also walked. The shore was nasty gravel and shortly before dark we made a fire and prepared our supper. Then the Bishop ordered the Indians to prepare for us a decent camping place, which they did, halfway up a sandy hill. We lay down and fell asleep, but were soon awakened by heavy drops of rain. The sky had clouded up and it was pitch dark. About midnight the water was streaming down the hill under us. Having decamped to the upper side of the stump of a large tree, I called the Bishop to come and join me, which after some persuasion he did. I showed him the way by striking a match from time to time. I was afterwards sorry for extending the invitation, as we soon discovered we had moved from bad to worse. However we remained in the mud and water until four in the morning, when I went down the hill and made a cup of tea on the fire of last night, which had kept alive under a large piece of log.

We left as soon as it was daylight. After a short walk along the beach we took to the bush, intending to make a short cut of a projecting point. After struggling about a couple of hours through the thick salal, we came to the Indian trail. We followed it with great avidity at about five miles an hour. To our great disappointment, we found that the trail led directly to our old camping place, where the fire on which we had cooked our breakfast was still smoking. Our courage now sank very low. Then, instead of following the same trail in the opposite direction, which with a little reflection we ought to have done, we went over rocks and boulders around the point, which we had intended to have cut off that morning.

According to directions given by the Clayoquots we were at a certain spot to cross to the Ucluelet Inlet. This we intended to do, when we took to the bush again. We walked and walked till I found my strength failing, which the Bishop noticed and proposed that we should take something to eat. We made a fire in the bush, and then we boiled doughnuts! We ate them with great appetite. At this point, the two Kyuquot Indians began to show bad will, and insisted on going back to the beach, which we did.

Early in the afternoon, the rain, which had fallen in the morning in the shape of a scotch mist, became thicker and thicker and, having come to a small bay where driftwood was piled up in great quantity, we prepared a place where we could spend the night. We started a big fire, which soon spread to the trees around. In the morning I discovered that a hole was burned through one of my boots and that my cloak was badly damaged. The Bishop's clothing had also suffered to a certain extent through fire. We took as breakfast the last piece of meat we had left, and we made flapjacks with our last flour. After this we began to walk with renewed courage. About nine the Bishop took a fainting fit. He lay down on the rocks and asked if I had any food left. I took down the satchel which I had on my back, and after careful examination I found a few grains of sugar and a little flour in the corner of an old flour sack. This I gathered in a spoon and presented to His Lordship. He would not take any of it except after I had taken my share, saying that he did not know what would become of us in case I should also give out. We next noticed that the Indians were gathering mussels on the rocks and eating them with great relish. This we also did and raw mussels and salal berries were the only food which we took till we reached Captain Francis' place in Ucluelet next morning.

Captain Thornton could hardly recognize us. Seeing our condition and hearing of our long compulsory abstinence from food, he advised us not to take a full meal until we had, by eating very little at a time, prepared our stomachs for their usual functions. At the same time the Captain went into his store and gave us new pants and shoes. All our clothes had been reduced to rags in our attempt to travel through the brushwood.

Our experience from Clayoquot to Ucluelet had such an effect on our general condition that it took more than two weeks for us to recover our usual strength.

At Ucluelet we did nothing, as the Indians were all away to their salmon rivers. The young chief Wish Koutl took us to Ekool and some Ekoolthaht Indians went with us to Namukamis where we found the Indians under the influence of liquor.

Then we made arrangements with an Ekoolthaht Indian to take us to

Nanaimo, which he promised to do for six dollars. We had a pleasant trip up the Alberni Canal. Having left Ekool in the morning, we arrived in the afternoon at China River and called at the house of the miners but found them absent. As a sign of our passing the Bishop wrote on their door the fact of our calling and wished them success. That night we were received by Mr. Clark, who was then manager of the Johnston farm. He showed us some fine horses of which he had twenty-two; also some of his cattle, saying that he had a hundred and sixty head running all over the settlement. A Mr. Taylor was the only other settler.

Next day we went to visit the Opetchesahts where we were all well received. They were then living above the forks of the river. The Sheshahts were also on the river, but, as their Chief had refused to receive us the day before, we passed them by.

Next day we again commenced our walk to Qualicum, a delightful trip over the newly-made road. [13] At noon we were at the lake, which we crossed in a canoe, and then we walked to the East Coast side, where we arrived at 5.

Here we pitched our tent. On Sunday morning we found a canoe in the bush, and with paddles and a sail made from our tent, we travelled with great speed to Nanaimo where we were in time to hear the Protestant bells ring for evening service. We took passage on the steamer *Emma* the next day for Victoria, and arrived in Victoria on Tuesday morning at 2. We went ashore at once and astonished everyone by arriving in time to say Mass. For both of us it was a Mass of thanksgiving.

FIRST MISSION ESTABLISHED ON THE WEST COAST OF VANCOUVER ISLAND AT HESQUIAT

About the beginning of February 1875, I had just returned from a mission to Sitka, Alaska Territory, when I was notified by Right Reverend Bishop Seghers, D.D., to prepare myself and to be ready to go to Hesquiat and take charge of the West Coast Indians at the beginning of the Spring.

In conformity with this order I got everything in readiness, and a carpenter was hired by His Lordship at the same time. Reverend Father Rondeault, of Quamichan, was requested to accompany us to Hesquiat and to help us put up the Mission buildings.

We left Victoria on the Feast of the Ascension, May 6, at five in the morning, on the sloop *Thornton*, owned by Captain Warren & Co. She was commanded by Captain George Brown. We had on board three small calves, one bull and two heifers, which were destined to become the pioneer cattle in this part of the country. A young Newfoundland dog was to be my only domestic companion after Noel Leclaire, the carpenter, and Reverend Father Rondeault finished the work for which they were sent. We had a rather quick passage as, having left Victoria on Thursday and called and discharged freight at Ekool, we arrived in Hesquiat Harbour next Tuesday afternoon. Off Clayoquot Sound we met two Hesquiat canoes on their way to Victoria, with Matlahaw, the Chief, and his father, in one of them. Although requested by Captain Brown to return with us, and offered a free passage on the schooner, they insisted on continuing their trip to Victoria.

After casting anchor in the inner harbour the weather became very stormy. This prevented us from landing our freight until Thursday morning. We had, however, put ashore our little calves immediately upon arriving. On Thursday when we walked over to the Hesquiat village, they followed us like dogs, sometimes forgetting themselves when amidst good pasture, and then running up to us with the utmost speed.

There was now the question of selecting a spot for our Mission buildings. The Chief was absent, and not an Indian dared or was willing to point a suitable place out to us. Every one of my suggestions were for various reasons repudiated and we owe it to Captain Brown that the Mission was put up where it now stands.

Our orders had been to put up a church of 60 x 26 feet and a small residence for the priest. Everything was to be done as cheaply as possible, as the establishment of a Mission was only an experiment. Later on, say five years, if the Mission was successful, more substantial buildings would be put up.

In December of the preceding year the bark *Edwin*, Captain Hughes, loaded with lumber for Australia, had become water-logged in the Straits. She had split open so as to make of her a complete wreck. The Captain's wife, now buried at Itloune, Hesquiat Harbour, had been crushed between the heavy timbers and his two little boys washed overboard as well as the Chinese cook.

Early one morning the Hesquiat Indians saw the vessel with all sails set taking the direction of Itloune before a southeasterly wind. Close to the vessel was a raft on which they noticed the sailors trying to make for shore and in great danger of being lost. Matlahaw, the chief of the tribe, suggested the propriety of going to the rescue of the drowning men. Several canoes were launched and off they went over the heavy and

Clayoquot beach camp.

35

stormy waves. They succeeded in taking off all the men. Matlahaw afterward received, from the Dominion government, a silver medal and from the United States government a liberal reward for himself and the men who had given any assistance to the ship-wrecked sailors.

The bark was now on the beach outside of Itloune Point and all the lumber, consisting of rafters, heavy and light, rough lumber and flooring, was piled up by the sea a mile along the shore. It was from the lumber of the unfortunate vessel that our Mission buildings were constructed. Captain Warren bought the wreck and from him we got almost all the lumber required. Some Indians had used part of it to construct new houses. After some trouble and reasoning they were prevailed upon to let us have the use of it all.

I may here state that the Indians had treated the sailors and Captain of the bark with much kindness. They appear, however, to have been a rough crowd. It seems hardly credible, still the rescuers maintain that when they arrived with their canoes alongside of the raft where most of the men were nearly perishing from cold and exposure, they were told to leave one of the crew. He was left, as I was afterwards told, because he was a Dutchman.

Later they began quarrelling in the Chief's house, fought and wounded each other to such an extent that they had to be separated and made to lodge in different houses. As soon as the weather permitted, the Indians took the men to Clayoquot Sound. From there they reached Ucluelet and were taken on one of Captain Spring's schooners to Victoria.

Immediately after landing, we set to work. We began by building a small shed, where we had our beds, stove, provisions, and where we took our meals. My dog slept under the bed, and the calves alongside the stove. Under one of the beds we had a barrel of beer, presented to us by Stuart & Keast of Victoria. At regular times the builders were invited to take a cup of the beverage, which they called "a cup of tea," when the Indians were present.

Although this was the best season of the year, the weather was most unpropitious, and before long our carpenter complained of being sick. Afterwards he tried to make a row and when told that we could do without him he managed to get better, but for whole days we could not get him to speak a word. Everything considered, the first Mission buildings on this coast were put up amidst much unpleasantness.

The first Mass was said in the new church on the fifth of July, it being the feast of the Most Precious Blood. All the Hesquiats were present; also, the Chief and a crowd of Muchalat Indians. Next morning a canoe took Reverend Father Rondeault and Leclaire to Victoria, and I was left alone in this place and in charge of all the Indians from Pachena to Cape Cook.

I soon discovered that the work before me was an uphill undertaking. To mention one fact only, there was not one Indian in Hesquiat who could act as interpreter. However, I managed to teach the tribe the "Catholic Ladder." And I made up my mind to study the language, which I found no easy matter, for I had no books to consult and there was no one who could give me any information about it.

In the beginning of August I made a trip to the Checklesets and other tribes on the way. Guyer, a Clayoquot, a first-rate interpreter, accompanied me and six Hesquiats, all full-grown men. The Indians would not allow their sons to go along for fear they might be killed by the Kyuquots, who were supposed to be very badly disposed to their tribe.

Hesquiat Church.

37

Guyer had some time before this stabbed a man belonging to Becher Bay, near Victoria. This man and his wife were slaves in Clayoquot and belonged to Chief Sheouse. This last, fearing trouble, asked Guyer to kill the man-slave, which he did, stabbing him in the chest with an ordinary file.

This misdeed weighed very heavy on the mind of Guyer. And he told me his reason for coming to Hesquiat and accompanying me on this trip was to seek relief for his mind. He wanted me to state that no harm would happen to him by the white man's police. I could not do so, and he begged me to take him, as soon as convenient, to the authorities in Victoria. The remorse of conscience of that man, or the dread of retaliation, was a real suffering to him.

At Nootka we found a young woman belonging to Ehattesaht, who was supposed to be the wife of one of the Nootka young men. She sent an Indian to see me, and wanted an interview. I allowed her the privilege. She told me that she wanted to accompany us to Ehattesaht. She would not live with the man who claimed her as his wife and she had been stolen by him out of a canoe against her will. She had been a slave in Nootka, and was considered as such again.

After considering these and other reasons and hearing the opinion of some of the influential Nootka Indians, I gave her permission to accompany us. The next day she was returned to her friends and home.

But nothing else unusual happened, although at Kyuquot we were very badly received. My Indians, suspecting danger, slept with knives in their hands. It was only after much trouble that they would allow me to baptize their children.

We were absent about two weeks and shortly afterwards I received a letter from Bishop Seghers summoning me to Victoria. I left Hesquiat about the twentieth of September and arrived back, on the schooner *Surprise*, on the fifth of October. Upon landing I was told that an Indian woman, "a doctoress," had died during my absence, after a few days' sickness. Next I heard that a large number of Nootka Indians were sick and several had died. The report arrived that the sickness was smallpox. The whole tribe was wild with excitement that they would come to Hesquiat and kill as many of the tribe as had died of the disease! I spurned the threat and persuaded the Indians not to be uneasy.

On the eighteenth of October the wife of Matlahaw died rather suddenly at Hesquiat. As I suspected that everything was not right, I assembled the Indians on the hill, and told those who were living in the Chief's house to move. Also, if there was anybody else unwell, to come and give me information. Upon arriving home, I was met by Charley, whose mother had died during my absence. He reported that his father was sick. I went to his house and found the old man very sick, evidently with smallpox. He was lying in one corner of the room and in the other corner was his sister, an elderly woman, also in the last stages of the fatal disease. I baptized both of them, saw them well provided with food and water and went home convinced that a very trying time was before me.

I was not disappointed, for next morning the first news I heard was that both were dead and that others had been taken sick. As soon as Mass was over, a large number of Indians came to my house and I made preparations to have the dead buried. I went and dug two graves, but when the time for the funeral had arrived no one would help me take away the corpses. I reasoned and entreated my visitors to give me a hand, but all to no purpose. At last, after several hours of talking, a Cape Flattery Indian, living with his Hesquiat wife, volunteered. Others followed his example, and I mustered a force of ten to the burying of the dead. Never was such a funeral seen by mortal man! First I had to give medicine to every one of them. As I had none, I boiled water, broke some biscuits in it, sweetened the whole with sugar, and insisted that this would be the very best preservative in the world against smallpox.

Then began the march. I led the procession, then came the ten in a line, with their faces blackened and covered with Indian charms. They were shouting and jumping, and when we came to the house where the dead were, not one dared to come in and assist me. But the Cape Flattery Indian again gave an example of bravery. He was accompanied by Charley's father-in-law and Charley himself. The coffin was a small canoe, to which was attached about forty feet of rope. We took up the old man first. He presented a ghastly sight as the blood and bloody matter covered his face and streamed out of his mouth. The woman was covered with two new black blankets and had evidently died first. Her brother had rendered to his dead sister the pious duty of clothing the corpse. She was put into the same canoe, and then orders were given to take hold of the lines. Everyone wanted to take the very end, but after some confusion the canoe was pulled out of the house. I acted the steersman for a good distance into the bush. After securely covering the original coffin with Indian planks, we all returned to my house.

Before entering, the Indians all rushed into the river praying and shouting. Having thrown away their blankets, which were their only covering, they next came in, everyone of them as naked as the moment he had been born. Some thoughtful woman, after some time, came with a supply of blankets and the spectacle became rather more decent and respectable.

Next day I went to see the Chief's daughter who was very low with smallpox. She was a courageous woman and did not give up till she was quite blind and her head as black and as thick as a large iron pot. She was baptized and seemed to be in the best disposition. Her own father and another old Indian helped me to bury her. The sight of the corpse was simply horrible, and as we left the shanty in which she died swarms of flies surrounded us all.

At this time, Matlahaw, the Hesquiat Chief, his father Townissim,

A group of Indians with their chief, Matlahaw.

40

Omerak and Charley had obtained permission to sleep in the Indian room of my house. Upon according this privilege, Matlahaw promised and gave me all the strip of land between the river and the beach.

I passed most of my time in vaccinating the Indians and in trying to cheer them up, for the fear and discouragement in some cases were altogether alarming. Matlahaw and Charley were hardly alive. Hence they would sit for hours together, telling me of the importance of their lives and insisting upon my using all possible means to preserve them from the disease. Charley had been vaccinated successfully in Victoria. Although I tried it twice on Matlahaw, the vaccine had no effect. This seemed to increase his fear. He now became morose and avoided the company of his friends. In fact he was not to be seen in the daytime for several days.

He used to be up before daylight and two or three mornings, as I got up, upon looking through my window, I noticed him sitting alongside of his father, apparently engaged with him in very secret conversation.

On the twenty-seventh of October he shot some blue jays in my potato patch. The rest of the time he stood outside, watching my movements, and from time to time exchanging a few words with the Indians who were constantly about my house. Towards evening the report that an Indian woman was very sick was received. I went to see her, but noticed that her case was not very serious yet. However, next morning the first thing I did upon getting up was to go and see the old woman, who was, if anything rather better than the day before.

After I had returned to my house and was about to go and ring the bell for Mass, Matlahaw came into my house and asked me for the loan of my gun. Upon handing it to him, I said it was unloaded. He simply remarked that he had powder and shot in his shanty, which was made of a few Indian planks and which with my permission he had constructed behind my little barn.

All the Indians of the tribe, save the old woman who had smallpox and Matlahaw and his father, were at Mass. The old man was missed at once. Afterwards it was found out that he had crossed the bay with his little grandchild and gone up Sydney Inlet, where his wife had gone before him. There she and her female slave died of smallpox. The old Chief, in a fit of passion, took a stone and with it killed the husband and one old slave. When the Mass was over, and just as I was finishing my breakfast, Charley came into my room and said, "Lookout, Leplet,[14] Matlahaw is sick. You had better take your gun from him." I made one or two inquiries, and after saying a few words jokingly, to give heart and courage to the messenger, who looked alarmingly excited or downhearted, I went out, my pipe in my mouth, to see the would-be patient.

When I arrived inside of his shanty, I noticed in the middle a small fire, before which he was squatting down. He had on his Chief's hat and also the coat presented by the Superintendent of Indian Affairs. Behind him, against the wall, stood my double-barrelled gun and an Indian musket. I asked what the matter was, when, smilingly, he looked up, and pulling the skin of his leg, answered, "Memaloose [15] -- smallpox." I assured him, saying that I would give him medicine and that by evening he would be all right, Again he looked up, his face being very pale and the sinews of his cheeks trembling, and pulling at the skin of his throat he repeated, "memaloose". Once more I repeated that I would give him medicine and that he would be well before evening.

Then I asked him to hand me my gun, which he took without getting up. Then pointing it towards me he explained, as I understood, that one of the barrels was not loaded. The fact of the muzzle of the gun being pointed straight to my face and noticing caps on both nipples and the cocks pulled up caused me instinctively to turn away my head, when lo! the explosion took place and blood spurted from my hand. The smoke was so thick that I could not see the would-be murderer. Thinking the whole affair to be an accident, after calmly remarking that I was shot in the hand, I walked down to the little river where I bowed down to bathe my wounds in the stream. Matlahaw shot again. This time he hit me in the right shoulder and all over my back.

I now knew the man wanted to kill me and I ran off to my house, where I found no one. Then I ran to the rancherie and was met by nearly all the men of the tribe to whom I told what had happened. Some of them pretended that the Moachats had done the shooting. After stating again and again that it was Matlahaw they became convinced that he indeed was the guilty party. After a few moments a film came over my eyes and thinking that I would not survive, I knelt down and said my acts of faith, hope, charity and contrition. Then I got up, went to my house and wrote on a piece of paper the name of the man who had shot me, put the paper in my bureau, locked it and put the key into my pocket. By this time the noise and alarm outside of my house was deafening. The loyal men of the tribe were there with axes and guns to kill their Chief. But he had run away into the bush and had not been seen after the shooting, save by an old woman.

Meanwhile I had been divested by some savages of my coat and underclothing. The Indians, upon noticing the blood, lost courage and one after the other walked out of the room, announcing to their friends that I was dying. This was also my opinion, although I felt no pain whatever, either in the hand or the back. I lay down and ordered cold dressing to be placed over my wounds. I noticed very little of what was going on, thinking that the best thing I could do was to pray and prepare myself to die.

Early the next day, October 29, two canoes, fully manned, left Hesquiat. The first went to Hot Springs Cove, where the sister of Matlahaw was residing with her Indian husband. The Indians, excited over the doings of her brother had decided to bring her home. In due time the canoe came back and the girl was landed on the beach before my house. She knew not what was in store for her. She knew not that as she was left there alone, crying, the Indians were plotting her death in expiation of what her brother had done to me. Such, however, was the case. When the plan was well prepared an elderly man came rushing into my house where I lay on my bed. He wanted my opinion, as the Indians were going to kill her. As the savage spoke his hair stood on end, froth was on his lips and his members trembled with excitement. I gave orders to have the young woman removed to a place of safety and to have her taken proper care of. I appointed one of the chiefs, a relative of hers, to act as her guardian during this time of unusual excitement.

The other canoe came back next day. She had gone to Clayoquot where a man, Fred Thornberg, had charge of a small trading post. This man was living with an Indian woman. When the Indians with the message called at his place, he met them with a Marlin rifle and would not allow them inside until he was fully convinced that his visitors were Hesquiat Indians. As his neighbours, that is the Indians of Clayoquot and Clayoquot Sound, were not to be trusted, he advised the Hesquiats to avail themselves of the darkness of the night to return to their homes. He sent a number of yards of calico (with his compliments and condolences) to be used by the Indians as a shroud for my "corpse."

On November 1, Monday at noon, a deputation of Indians excitedly entered my house and told me that they were going to send a canoe with the news of my state to Victoria, and report to the Bishop and the police. I told them quietly to please themselves, but, as they were determined to leave at once, I gave them a paper on which I had written a few words every morning. 16

Meanwhile my wounds became more and more inflamed. The Indians were up with me day and night, constantly pouring cold water over my injured hand. The wound in my back and side gave me great pain because I had to lie on them and they could not be reached by cold water dressings. As the hours and days advanced the swelling increased and inflammation was rapidly gaining. I was trembling with cold, although the Indians kept up a good fire. At last, on Tuesday, the 9th, just as it was getting dark, an Indian ran into my house out of breath and shouted that a man-of-war was entering the harbour.

I cannot describe my feelings and those of the poor Indians who were in my room and acted as nurses. Half an hour later, Dr. Walkem, who had volunteered to come to my assistance, rushed into my room. After examining my hand he expressed the opinion that it could not be saved and that I would have to submit to amputation. By that time Bishop Seghers, God bless him, had also come in. I can see him now, a picture of sadness. With tears in his eyes he told me how happy he felt to find me alive ... I could hardly utter a word. My strength was gone. I had not tasted food or drink for several days.

Frederick Thornberg, his daughter and two sons aboard the *Libbie* in 1907.

44

The Bishop went into my bedroom, opened a bottle of port wine and gave me a dose of the medicine, as he called it, in the presence of the natives and lo! my strength and courage came back at once. I told them of the details of my situation since I had seen him a month before in Victoria.

The doctor of the Navy, Dr. Redfern, after thoroughly examining my wounds, declared that nothing could be done at present. I would have to go to the hospital in Victoria, and he urged upon me the propriety of taking some food. He then cooked a meal. Although everything was prepared in an artistic shape, I could not take more than one or two mouthfuls.

Next morning Captain Harris of the H.M.S. *Rocket* came on shore and proposed to have the would-be murderer arrested. In fact he stated that it was part of his object in coming to Hesquiat. But just then an Indian came into my house with the news of new cases of smallpox, and expressed his uneasiness and that of his Indian friends to be left alone with the dread disease in the village. Happily, Captain Harris did not understand the messenger. So we urged upon him the necessity of returning to Victoria, as the doctors insisted that my wounds would have to be attended to without further delay. Besides, I told him, the man who had shot me had run away into the bush. He had not been seen since and that he might be ten or twenty miles away in the mountains. An arrangement was then made with the principal men of the tribe that they were to take Matlahaw to Victoria in case he could be arrested. The Provincial Police would pay them for their trouble the sum of $100, and a supply of provisions.

Thereupon arrangements were made to have me conveyed on board of the man-of-war. Eight men placed me on a cot, took me down to the beach between two lines of Indians, whilst one of the chiefs made a speech regretting what had occurred and bespeaking the speedy return of "their priest". When we arrived at the vessel, the cot was slung from the spanker-boom and an awning was stretched over the whole. I was made to feel as comfortable as possible under the circumstances.

We arrived in Victoria next morning. At the time of our landing an immense crowd of people were on the wharves. The city was in great excitement. The news had just reached the people that the steamship *Pacific* with 260 passengers -- quite a number of Victorians -- had foundered at sea and that thus far only one passenger had reached shore alive.[17] As we came from the very coast where the wreck had taken place, and as it had happened just a day before, the people were all in hopes that a number might have been picked up at sea. We had seen nothing of the wreck, and the crowd, looking for friends and good news, were doomed to return home disappointed.

The same men who had taken me in a cot on the man-of-war carried me on their shoulders from the vessel to the Bishop's residence, and then landed me on a table in the dining room. The room -- where I had passed so many pleasant hours with Bishop Demers and Bishop Seghers, his successor, and my colleagues, the priests of the diocese and especially of the Cathedral -- now looked gloomy. Everyone wanted to have a look and say a good word. The Sisters of St. Ann were there -- also well represented. Warm water, towels, linen and other necessary articles were prepared by them, and the doctors, four in number, began to talk business.

They were going to amputate the hand. Perhaps it would do to amputate only the two first fingers? I heard them make this and other remarks. However, I was not going to part with those necessary members of a priest's body to allow him to say Mass without an objection. And object I did. I asked them to allow me to die rather than have me become a useless man in the world, such as a priest would be if he cannot say Mass. Protestants as they were, the doctors, at first, did not understand my reiterated pleadings to be allowed to keep my hand and fingers. However, they concluded to wait a couple of days and for the time being agreed among themselves to cut open the main ulcers, remove the broken bones and cut off pieces of lead and other foreign matter.

They left me with the expectation of returning a couple of days later to perform the amputation, but prayer had the best of them. Two days later one of the doctors made his usual call. Seeing the blood had begun again to circulate, he could not conceal his astonishment and went away wondering how this unexpected change could have occurred. I was in the doctors' hands for nearly five months. I then heard that a schooner was advertised to go out sealing to the west coast. Foreseeing that no other opportunity to return to my mission would offer for the next six months, I asked for a passage on board and departed for Hesquiat on March 23, 1876.

I arrived in Hesquiat on April 5. The Indians learned that I was on my way back to the Mission. Understanding that the vessel on which I had embarked would not come as far as their village, they sent a canoe with nine men to meet me and take me home. I met them at Asatikis, about twenty miles from the Mission. On our way we called at Marktosis and baptized the newly-born children. Next day we arrived at Hesquiat.

My house was in the state I had left it -- the floor covered with blood. The temporary bunk which I had caused to be put up in my sitting-room, so as to have more space to move about with water, dressings, etc., was still there. Everything reminded me of sad days and sleepless nights. It all had a tendency to make me feel downhearted, but the Indians were so happy to see me back that I put aside all other thoughts. After a few days' cleaning, settling down again, I recommenced my work where I had left it off.

On Easter Sunday I established a force of policemen. The occasion had been furnished by the Indians themselves. They had resolved to have a feast in my honour and to present me with a gift of their own as a sign of their good feelings towards me. True enough, the day was appointed and two influential men of the tribe were delegated to come and invite me. The men were dressed up in red blankets over their red skins, pants and shirts being an unknown article to men of their class. Their faces were covered with black and red paint, and bird down covered their heads and their long hair. They shouted rather than spoke, at the same time giving vent to wild, savage gesticulations.

And so I went to the feast, which was given in one of the houses of a chief. As there were no chairs in the village a thoughtful savage took one of my own and placed it in the middle of the immense building.

Hesquiat Mission.

47

There I sat like an Indian chief, calmly smoking my pipe and pretending to enjoy everything that was going on. There was dancing and gesticulations, and many other extravagant things. No one can fancy this who has not seen wild men and women, covered with feathers and with painted cheeks, giving free expression to the feelings of their savage heart and nature. This sort of thing lasted for about two hours. Being nearly blind with the smoke of the campfires and as nearly deaf with the noise made by the women, as they beat with sticks on planks and Indian boxes to the measure of the songs of the men and boys and the younger class of women, I was anxious to go home and enjoy fresh air and peace. But what should happen? There in a corner got up one of the chiefs and taking a shawl from a woman's shoulders, held it open in view of the whole tribe and looking at me as with an angry countenance he called out, "Leplet, Leplet, -- Priest, Priest, -- this is for you, this is for you. I present it to you in the name of the tribe of the Hesquiats, who are all present here to do honour to you."

I do not know what anybody else would have done; as for me, I took the shawl and thanked the tribe and went home. Scarcely had I reached my house when I began to reflect and ask of myself, "What in the world shall I do with the shawl?" After mature reflection, I hit upon a plan to get rid of it.

Easter Sunday arrived and, as said above, I established a force of Indian policemen, as asked for by the Indians themselves and approved by the Bishop. Having then carefully selected my men I proceeded between high Mass and evening service to the house of one of the chiefs where the whole tribe was assembled. I explained to them the object of the meeting. I then appointed three men to act as Indian constables, and gave each of them coat and pants, to distinguish them from other savages and as a mark of their authority. Then taking the shawl, I held it up before the tribe and made a present of it to the woman who took care of the orphan boy of the man who had tried to kill me. The new policemen were appointed guardians of the future chief of the Hesquiats. I availed myself of this season of fervor to teach them the "Catholic Ladder" of Father Lacombe. I also taught them to sing Mass in plain chant.

On June 5 there was unusual excitement in the village. Early in the morning news was brought that a dead whale is floating off the harbour. There is shouting and running about; paddles are got ready and all the large canoes pulled down to the beach. Not an able-bodied man is left on shore; even a number of women accompany the crowd. You can see the excitement at sea, you can hear the shouting and singing as the monster of the deep is being towed toward the shore. At last shore is reached. The men stand up in their canoes, paddles in hand, and intone one of their old songs. The women on shore stand alongside the houses, and taking part in the general rejoicings, beat a measure on the sides of the dwellings and their old Indian drums.

As the day is well advanced, it is decided that the cutting up of the whale shall be postponed until next morning. Meanwhile knives are prepared, and the chiefs and principal men who alone are entitled to a share of the big fish, secure a number of inferior men to give them a hand next day.

June 6. — Long before daylight the whale is surrounded by half-naked Indians. They all know the share they have a right to, but not one seems satisifed with what belongs to him — there is no end of quarreling and pushing each other about. In the disturbance a couple are wounded — one very seriously. After half a day of fighting and general disturbance, the whale being cut up, the Indians all retire to their houses, happy at the prospect of enjoying the delicacies of whale blubber and whale oil for the next few months.

June 7. — In the heat of their happiness the chiefs decide to go to Ahousat and invite their friends of that tribe to come and have a share in the general festivities.

June 10. — Three Ahousaht canoes arrive in Hesquiat, in all twenty men. All the Indians assemble to receive their guests on the beach. They walk in procession, one man behind the other, in white man's clothes, save two, whose heads are covered with feathers, and who dance the dances usual on such occasions. Meanwhile the Ahousahts, appreciating the compliment, rise in their canoes, beat a measure on the sides of the canoes, and sing a song in response to a speech made by one of the Hesquiats.

It all finishes by the pulling up of the canoes of the visitors and leading them into the house of one of the chiefs, who at once entertains them at a meal of whale meat. The accidental floating on shore of this whale and the importance which the Indians attach to this event had caused them to talk a great deal about the subject. Apropos of this event, let me give a notion of their superstitions on this point.

A few months ago an old Indian Chief, called Koninnah and known all along the coast, died in Hesquiat. This man enjoyed the reputation of bringing dead whales, almost at will, to the shores of the Hesquiat. Even now he gets the credit for the whale that floated on shore yesterday. For the Indians say that their chiefs do not forget their friends and subjects when they reach the other world. Hence, Koninnah, by his influence, sent them a dead whale as a token of good-will.

This man, I am told, had here in the bush a small house made of cedar planks. To this house he would retire from time to time to visit his charms, and go through his devotions, prayers and incantations. His charms mostly consisted of human skeletons, especially those of ancient chiefs and famous hunters. To these skeletons he would speak as if they were alive and order them to give him a whale. Each of the skeletons had its turn. In addressing himself to them he would give due credit to those of their number who, he had reason to suspect, had been granting his request.

It is narrated that Koninnah one day was boasting of causing a dead whale to strand in Hesquiat Harbour. As it happened, the flesh was tough and the oil not sweet. The Indians found fault with their supposed good luck so Koninnah told them that he would get another one for them of better quality: a couple of days later his prediction was verified.

The Indians tell their yarns with such conviction of truth that it is almost painful to have to contradict them.

Koninnah, when desirous to be successful, led a life of strict continence. He also observed laws of fasting and bathing in salt water. Besides, he was never to taste the flesh or blubber of his whales under pain of losing his extraordinary powers. Whales are an article of immense importance in this locality and with all the tribes of the coast. They are considered the best and most wholesome food, and the oil is used with all kinds of dry fish.

June 23. — Up to this date it has rained a great deal. The weather now seems to have broken and a rainbow is seen in the direction of Sydney Inlet. At once a couple of Indians to whom I am talking bow their heads and turn their backs on the rainbow. I learn from them that the Indians on the coast never look at a rainbow for fear that some harm befall them.

June 25. — A child was born today and, being the offspring of an important man, there is great rejoicing. According to an old custom a couple of men having the title *Okhei* [18] — beggars — covered with feathers and paint, go to the happy parents' house and there begin their pranks and dances accompanied by singing and pleading. Their only object was to induce the child's father to make presents to them and invite the tribe to a feast of food and amusements. Strange to say, the father of the newly-born child is confined to the house as well as the mother — on no pretext can he go outside and look at the ocean or sky.

Such conduct on his part would have the effect to scare away the fish and to anger the waves of the sea. In case of extreme need to go outside, the man must cover his eyes and look down to find his way; under no pretext can he look up or walk along the beach.

Apart from the general rejoicings, the old women of the neighbourhood must also have their turn. There they sit around the newly-born with sticks in their hands and, striking up some of their usual

Reverend Father Brabant, ca. 1877. Notice the deformation of the fingers of his right hand — the result of Matlahaw's attack.

songs, begin to beat time on cedar boards or a worn-out tambourine. This they continue until the new mother or her nearest relatives makes some suitable present to all the women visitors.

The name of the infant, given before birth, is that of a dead female relative or ancestor. In case the progeny belongs to the masculine gender another name is soon substituted.

Another peculiarity about the Indians is this; if anyone dies his name dies with him. No one will dare pronounce it again, especially in the presence of relatives, and if anyone in the tribe has a name which sounds like that of the deceased he will change it at once. There is something so ludicrous about this that today you may know the names of all your people, and six months later you are likely to know only half of them. Christian names are a great improvement, but in giving them one must be careful to make a proper choice. The Indians cannot pronounce all our letters. A boy called Damien was the other day asked his name, to which he replied, without showing any signs of anger, "Dam You."

The names given by the Indians to their children are family names; that is, they belong especially to a certain clan of the whole tribe. Through intermarriage, however, many have passed into different clans, and in fact, as far as I can see, they now are pretty well spread all over the tribe. Inferior people dare not give to their children certain names, which seem to be the property of the chiefs of the different tribes, nor do they, whatever their merits may be, apply them to themselves.

In general, the names of our Indians have some meaning, being mostly suggested by the doings of some big hunter or ancient warrior. Quite a number of them, though, have no meaning whatever. They are simply given as having been the name of some ancestor. As a rule, children take the name of their grandfather or grandmother, sometimes of other ancestors, but never those of their parents. I gather, from what I have heard, that respect for the dead and their living relatives seems to be the main reason for avoiding the adoption of their names or of having them pronounced within a certain period after their death.

June 26. — A canoe containing some nine Ekoolthahts just arrived. She attracted our attention from quite a distance at sea. Although the wind was favourable she took in her sail, when we could hardly see her. She carried a flag at her stern and the Indians were paddling as hard as they could. Next we could hear them sing, and when they were quite near shore they stopped paddling. One of the men got up and struck up a song in a loud, moaning tone. Then, upon landing, he shouted something to our people, which I was afterwards told was the name of our Chief, and gave him a couple of blankets as a present.

The Hesquiat Indians evidently knew the object of the visitors. As a rule, with all the tribes on the coast, when strangers arrive at a village, there are always a number of people who run down to the beach, either to welcome them or to get the news. In the present case, not one of our people went to meet the strangers, who were now at the landing place. Yet, when called upon to go and receive the blankets, the Chief sent one of the young men to fetch them to him. After this was done, the same spokesman of the strangers got up again. In the same tone of voice he called out the name of the second Chief and made him also a present of a couple of blankets, which a messenger went down to the beach to take for the second Chief. This was repeated six times, so that all the principal Chiefs received a present before the men put an end to the generosity.

Some of the Hesquiats, upon hearing the name of their sons called out by these strangers, got quite excited, and before inviting them into their houses also made presents to them, which were accepted with the usual expression of thanks, "Tlako! Tlako!"

It struck me strange that in all their feasts and meetings the parents are not mentioned. If a man invites someone to a feast, if he has an heir he will always extend the invitation to the name of that heir. Also, when presents are given, they are always given to the heir, even if he is only one day old. The parents always disappear behind the heir, who in all cases comes or stands to the front in the estimation of all the Indians on this coast.

The Indians of Ekool are here with the object of inviting the Hesquiats to a potlatch, as the peculiar way of their landing here indicates. This is the first invitation to a potlatch extended to my Indians since I came to the coast.

A potlatch, as I understand it from the meaning of the word, is a feast where gifts or presents are made, a gift-feast. The priests and ministers of all denominations condemn the feast, and the Dominion government, at their suggestion, has passed a law prohibiting it under certain penalties. As for me, I cannot see any harm in it, although I would rather have it abolished. I had no reason therefore of my own, but giving due importance to the conduct of men longer in the ministry than myself, I used all my influence to keep my people from going to the present gift-feast in Barkley Sound.

As I understand it, a potlatch simply consists of this; a man, say a chief of a certain tribe, after a season of prosperity has accumulated a

53

large number of blankets — the Indians here have no money. He then resolves to invite a neighbouring tribe to a feast and distribute to them according to their rank the fruit of his industry — his blankets. He privately warns the members of his own tribe to be prepared for the reception of the tribe which he singles out. This proposition is approved of, and his friends, the principal chiefs, secure the necessary provisions, so that when the feast is on they can entertain at a meal the invited guests.

The tribe to be invited are also warned in due time and afterwards formally notified that their presence is expected soon after the formal warning. The occasion of starting is one of great excitement. All the able-bodied men, as a rule, and also a number of women go along, and are evidently intent upon having a good time. The arrival at the village where they are invited is also very exciting. They sing and dance in their canoes, the drums beat and muskets are fired off. Meanwhile the people on shore are also doing their best to make a show. After many different ways of bidding welcome, the guests land and are invited by one of the chiefs to share his hospitality by taking a good meal. Immediately after this meal, and more frequently before it, the visitors are divided, for their present quarters during the day when disengaged and for sleeping at night. There they are also welcome at meals. But every day during their stay one or more of the chiefs or important men invite all the strangers to eat in their houses, where singing, dancing and exchanging gifts and presents are freely indulged in.

A potlatch or gift-feast consists in exchanging presents either with the object of gain or of exciting the admiration of their fellows. Sometimes in the height of his savage pride an Indian makes presents, for which he is afterwards sorry, especially if an article far below the value of the one he has himself made a present of is returned. Everyone seems to speculate either for gain or glory.

On the fourth or fifth day the feast comes to a conclusion. The man who has invited the strangers makes presents to all of them according to their rank or importance. He does not lose sight of the probability that the one to whom the presents are made will some time be able to make an equal return. Herein the potlatch fails of good. The old people are almost lost sight of and so are orphan children, especially those of the female gender. A potlatch is not an expression of charity, but a pure piece of speculation.

During the festivities, the Indians wear their best blankets and keep themselves cleaner than usual, but for their dances and games, they resort to all means to make themselves look ugly or odd: their faces painted, their heads covered with down, masks of different descriptions, bear skins are put on and even Chinese queues are worn by the younger class of people.

The festivities come to an end by a speech made by the one who invited the strangers. These pack their gifts to their canoes and the people resume their usual work and occupations. The hospitality shown by our Indians to visitors or strangers is quite noteworthy. As soon as a canoe of strangers arrives at a village, they are at once invited by some of the residents to carry their belongings up to their house. A meal is prepared for them and lodgings are offered. When travelling, our people take little or no provisions, for they may always reckon upon receiving hospitality wherever they happen to go on shore near an Indian settlement. Whatever food is left after their meal is taken to the canoe of the visitors. It is used by them on their voyage home and remnants are distributed to their friends at home. During the partaking of this food, all the news of interest is communicated.

In their own homes, after a successful day or season at fishing or hunting, invitations are often sent out to the tribe or a part thereof, to come and partake of a feast, the remnants, in all cases, being carried by the young people to the respective homes of the invited guests. Before retiring a speech is made by one of the principal men, and thanks are duly given to the host in the name of those who are invited. In all cases the invited guests occupy a place according to their rank. It reminds one very much of the customs of the Jews at the time of our Lord.

June 28. — Today the first funeral according to the rites of the Catholic Church took place. A funeral is never a very funny affair; still this one seems to be an exception, at least as far as I was concerned. The man died about midnight. As was customary he was put in a box or trunk at once, a fact of which I was warned by a messenger. I got up and told the Indian that the funeral could not take place before morning. However, there was no objection to having the corpse put outside of the house. About three I was again aroused. Once more I told the messenger to have patience until Mass. But about four there were quite a number of messengers. I got up again; by this time the primitive coffin was in evidence at the church door. Still, I thought it rather unusual to bury the dead at four in the morning. So I postponed it again. When five came there was no use trying to put it off any longer. The funeral was to take place right then. Quite a number of people crowded into the church; the coffin was put in the centre, but everyone faced the coffin. Even those in front in the church turned their backs to the altar. When Mass was over I solemnly headed the funeral procession with cross and altar boys, reciting the prayers of the Ritual. Looking behind me, I noticed that the savages had taken another road with the corpse. In fact they had put it into a canoe and were paddling across the small bay around which I was walking. Still, we arrived ultimately at the same spot, but to my dismay there was no grave dug. Shovel and pick were sent for. I took off my surplice, began the digging, got a man to continue and went home and had my breakfast. When everything was ready, I went back and blessed the grave and the first Christian of this region was laid to rest in consecrated ground. R.I.P.

I am informed that this Christian funeral is quite a victory towards breaking up the old pagan customs and superstitions, in case of sickness and death. First of all, because the Indian was really dead when he was removed and put into the coffin. Many instances are narrated where people have been buried alive. A coasting trader told me that when he was stationed at Clayoquot a man was put on an island where there was a small trading post. During the night, somebody rapped at his door. He got up and there stood a naked Indian, the man who had been buried the day before. He lived two years after his supposed death. The strangest part of the story was that the Indians who had buried him maintained that the man was dead, and that it was a bad spirit that now occupied the corpse, or rather the body of the new Lazarus.

Sometime ago I was called to see a man supposedly dying. What was my horror when coming in the house I found them tying together his arms and legs and actually preparing to bury him alive.

A young married woman had given birth to her first child. She had convulsions and fainted away. No time was lost in putting her in a box, and removing her into a cave close to the village. Next morning a man went bathing in the neighbourhood and heard the poor girl cry for pity. She was alive and, horrible to relate, she was left to die in her misery. Her new-born baby soon followed her in death, having starved for want of food. This happened at Nootka. I know a man whose son, the father of a small family, took sick through exposure. He seemed to have cramps all over his body and became speechless. After four or five days the old man ordered a coffin to be made and asked the services of three young men — they narrated this to me themselves with delight — to force the sick son into the box. They tied his hands and feet, and having him well secured they did as they were told by the heartless father, and took him into the bush to perish of misery. During all this transaction, the unfortunate fellow groaned and seemed to ask them to have pity on him. They were inclined to comply with his wishes, but they were told,

"Never mind, do as I tell you. My son is dead. The bad spirit has hold of him and makes all this resistance."

In rare instances the Indians mutilate the bodies of the dead before removing them. In one case, a young couple had had several children, but they had all died soon after birth. This happened again, and the father, upon the advice of the old people, and with the object that such misfortune should not happen again, literally broke every bone of the legs and arms of the dead infant.

The Indians up to this time had never buried their dead underground. When it was time to remove a corpse, they made an opening in the side of the house. The children and younger people, the savages think, will die if they pass through the passage made by people carrying out a corpse. By removing a few of the side boards of their houses, they made a hole to carry out the dead. Then they walk, if possible, on the beach below the high water mark. If the body was placed in a canoe, that canoe was afterwards destroyed. The bodies were removed only a small distance from the village and placed in a prominent place on the limbs of trees, ten or twenty feet from the ground. There they were fastened to the trunk of the tree with strong cords made of cedar bark. Afterwards they were covered with blankets and then a display was made by hanging blankets all around.

While this was going on, the people in the house, especially the old women, gathered everything that had belonged to the dead man or woman and threw all the relics into a fire outside. Whatever was not inflammable, they destroyed, and you could hear them in the houses cry and lament and utter the most unearthly wailings that one can listen to.

When men of importance die, the mourning is general and the scenes enacted go beyond all limits. Those of a lower rank are mourned by only their own relatives and nearest friends. A year later the relatives and friends of the deceased walk all in a group to the tree where the body has been placed. There they open the box and taking out the skull they carry it to their house and there keep it as a relic. The idea is, I am told, to keep it from desecration. The skull of the dead is used as a charm for success as a hunter, warrior or a medicine man. Yet, not withstanding all the precautions that are taken, you can find along the streams different constructions that have been put up by the natives, where they used to go and pray for good luck or success. And there you invariably find the skull of some dead Indian.

July 10. — I arrived back from a trip along the coast with six of the best and strongest young men. We were well received by the different tribes and visited them all. The Checklesets we met in a small bay near Cape Cook, the extreme limit of the Mission of the Sacred Heart.

On our way back we called on the Ehattesaht Indians living near Tutchu. There we found Chief Maquinna, being on his father's side the Chief of his tribe and on his mother's side, the Chief of the Nootka or Moachat people.[19] We were ushered into his lodge by the Chief himself. His wife, the sister of Matlahaw, received us with evident signs of uneasiness and shame. However, I spoke to her kindly and my Indians also tried to make her feel at ease.

After giving Catechism instructions to all the Indians present, I went outside with the object of saying my office, and having retired to a certain distance from the camp, I felt annoyed to see Maquinna come and join me. I found an excuse to send him away for a few minutes, and availed myself of his absence to walk up a small creek where I could say my office without being disturbed. From there I saw my Hesquiat guides running around in a great state of excitement. They found me at last, and coming up they told me to quit my place of refuge and not to go out of their sight again. I knew not what they meant and followed their advice. When night came I prepared myself to lie down in the Chief's house, who had acted, as it struck me then, in a very suspicious way in the latter part of the afternoon. I went to sleep about 10, and expected to have a good night, for I was worn out with fatigue. The thick smoke of the open fire almost made me blind, and, although I was lying on the bare boards, I dozed off almost at once.

Suddenly I felt an oppression on my chest. I awoke and saw Maquinna's face close to mine. His eyes were staring out of their sockets, and his heavy breath was suffocating. What did he want? What was his intention or purpose?

Next morning, just at daylight, I was aroused from my couch by one of my crew. He told me to get up at once as quietly as possible and follow him out of the rancherie. I followed his orders, but not withstanding our precautions we were detected. We jumped into our canoe; Maquinna followed us in a rage down the beach and abused my people in the most insulting language. However, no notice was taken. My men were at their paddles and they did not take a breath till we were several miles away. Then, looking back and seeing we were not being followed, one of them told of our dangerous position the day before.

Maquinna was going to have me killed by one of his men if he could not succeed in doing it himself. Then he was going to accuse my guides of having committed the murder. This was in order to get even with them, for one of the men with me had taken Townissim to Victoria and delivered him to the police. There the old man had been accused of having incited his son to do the shooting. I was told that such a practice is very common with savages of this coast. Many a war has had its origin and cause in false accusations of this kind.

July 16. — Townissim, the father of Matlahaw, arrived in Hesquiat. Townissim was the chief of Hesquiat and Matlahaw was acting as his successor.

A few days after the man-of-war had taken me to Victoria, the Indians arranged a search party, and they had promised to take the young Chief to the authorities in case he could be found. All the able-bodied men took part, and having started from a certain point, they meant to walk through the bush for miles around. They had hardly begun their work when one of the party uttered a cry of alarm. They gathered together and to their horror they saw only a few paces away, the body of a dead man at the foot of a large, hollow tree.[20] There could be no mistake about it. He wore his uniform as chief and a medal presented by the Dominion government on his breast. Horrified, they all retired, gave the news to their friends, and looked upon the spot as a place to be avoided. However, before making this search they had already arrested Townissim, and taken him to Victoria. They accused him, and not without grave reason, of being at the bottom of all the trouble. Indeed, previous to the shooting, the old man had been seen for three successive mornings in close private conversation with his son. On the morning of the shooting he had left the village, even before daylight, taking along his grandchild, and had not been seen since. From this the Indians concluded that the man knew what was going to take place, and had kept out of the way till further developments.

Hence they had at once begun their search. One morning they had noticed the smoke of a camp at Entrance Point and had crossed in their canoes and arrested him. He was six months in jail in Victoria. When the news that Matlahaw was dead reached the authorities, he was sent back with a caution, and in due time he arrived in Hesquiat.

July 25. — Townissim came to my house today just as quite a number of Indians were in my house. I told them to be kind to him and at the same time told him to show no ill feelings against anybody.

August 23. — Notwithstanding my caution, Townissim is inciting the Indians against me. I heard that the poor man is in dread of being killed by his own subjects. Whenever he goes outside of his dwelling, he always carries a knife concealed in his blanket.

September 25. — Good news today. The Bishop is on his way to this place and is accompanied by a priest.

59

September 29. — Right Reverend C.J. Seghers, accompanied by Reverend P.J. Nicolaye, arrived in Hesquiat a few minutes before midnight.

October 1. — Feast of the Holy Rosary. The Bishop blessed our new church, the first on the west coast of Vancouver Island, and placed it under the patronage of St. Anthonine. A procession was organized in which all the Hesquiat participated, all the Muchalats, and a number of Nootka, Clayoquot and Ahousaht.

October 8. — The Hesquiat chiefs were called together and a grant of land was made, on which, in the distant future, it is proposed to build a substantial church. The ground may be taken up at once and cultivated.

October 10. — Reverend Father Nicolaye received leave to stay with me during the winter. He is supposed to prepare himself to take charge of a portion of my Mission next spring.

October 12. — The Bishop left on the schooner *Alert*, G. Brown Captain, and returned to Victoria. His visit to the Mission created quite an excitement amongst the Indians as he has told them that they must prepare for baptism. I avail myself of the opportunity to commence preaching against their superstitions with new zeal and determination.

At this time of the year many of our Indians go up the inlets and rivers with the object of making new canoes. Up on the hillsides or on the lowlands, they cut down a cedar tree. With a common axe they cut off a length according to the size required for the purposes of the canoe, i.e. sealing, fishing, sea otter hunting or travelling. Then they put the proper shape to it, very roughly, first outside, then inside. Next they invite some friends and together they pull the clumsy frame to the stream or to the ocean and float it to the village. When otherwise unemployed, especially in the early morning and toward evening, they use a peculiar hand chisel and adze and with wonderful patience they cut off chip after chip. The frame is reduced to the proper thickness, say one inch or more for the sides and double that for the bottom. The knot-holes are filled up and the finishing pieces put in. When all this is done, a fire is made under the canoe, which is raised up from the ground on blocks, and the bottom is rendered perfectly smooth. All the work is done without instruments to go by or measure. Yet most of these canoes are so true and so well shaped and proportioned that not even an expert could detect the least flaw or imperfection.

October 22. — All the natives of the tribe came to church today, even those living up the inlet or rivers. I made a rule in church that all the people, men, women and children, must at least wear a shirt. No one will be admitted into my house except if he wears a shirt under his blanket. After this I showed them the absurdity of some of their superstitions.

As this is the salmon season, the old people are as usual preaching to the tribe the propriety of conforming with the old established regulations, lest this great article of food should leave the neighbourhood and not come back again. For instance, salmon should not be cut open with a knife. They should not be boiled in an iron pot and not given as food to dogs or cats. The bones must be carefully collected and thrown into the sea. Under no consideration must salmon be given to any white man, including the priest, lest he prepare it in lard or in a frying pan. It should not be taken to the houses in baskets, but carried carefully one in each hand. These and many other details will show what an amount of absurdities are in these people's minds. It is almost humiliating to have to say that this and like matters formed the subject of my sermon today. It created quite a revolution in the camp and had the effect of my presence here becoming a cause of alarm, and a matter of regret on the part of the men and women in the village.

November 1. — For some time the Indians, in discussing with me their customs and beliefs, have been talking about a mountain said to be inhabited by a ghost or spirit.[21] It seems to be the main prop of their creed. It struck me that if I could not prove this to be a fraud, I could not hope to uproot the rest of their superstitions. Hence I resolved to visit the mountain, and show them that they had been deceived by their forefathers.

According to the legend, nine men have died on the top of that mountain through entering a cave, the home of the ghost, without having first made the requisite preparations. Some of these preparations are to be a ten day fast and abstinence from all relations with the other sex for ten months. The natives have an immense idea of continence and they attribute to the fact of my vow of chastity that I was not killed on the spot when their Chief shot me. In preparation for their wars, their hunting parties and every undertaking of great importance, they keep or pretend to keep strict continence.

The legend continues that only one man has entered the home of the ghost, and that he used to do so every year, in consequence of which he was the most successful in the whale hunt, an average catch being ten whales per season. His nine brothers begged to be allowed to accompany him on the hazardous expedition. After using every means to dissuade them, and seeing that they would insist, he at last complied with their request. The hero of the expedition insisted that the brothers should enter first into the supposed home of the ghost. One after the other entered as he was told; the tenth was just about to do so, when all of a sudden the entrance closed up. It remained closed until the nine unfortunate men had been torn to pieces and devoured by animals the size of a mink.

The hero of the story reported what had happened upon his arrival in the camp. Ever since that time the cave has been looked upon as a famous and sacred spot. The report adds that as soon as anybody approaches the top of the mountain pieces of rocks and pebbles are thrown at the visitor and the ghost is heard to groan from a distance. It also does this when a severe easterly storm approaches.

I have been obliged to manifest my plan in order to secure a crew to carry me to the foot of the famous mountain and, if willing, to accompany me to the top. This met with general disapprobation from the tribe. All the important men put their strength together, determined to prevent me from carrying out my plan. Consequently they came to my house, and by violent gesticulations and with shouts, declared that I cannot go. I am sure not to come back alive. Two young men who had promised to accompany me were deterred from doing so. Only one intrepid fellow kept his promise. The Indians threatened to kill him in case he does not bring me back alive. Seeing that all their efforts to prevent me were useless, they retired full of dissatisfaction and anger, assuring me that I will perish in the attempt. They think my fellow white men will blame them for having been indirectly the cause of my death.

Late in the evening an old man, in order to make up for the conduct of his son, who after promising to accompany me, had backed out, says he will be a member of our party. He adds that he will take along an axe to knock the ghost on the head.

November 2. — After offering up the Holy Sacrifice of the Mass, I warned the Indians that I would leave at once, and that I hoped no further resistance would be made. I took along Father Nicolaye who was very anxious to accompany us.

We arrived at noon at the foot of the mountain, called by the natives Kwoahall. We experienced very little or no difficulty in ascending it, for it was clear of brushwood and covered only thinly with cedar trees, some of which are remarkable for their size. At four we were at the foot of an immense bluff which crowns the mountain and which, to the southeast, is of a dark red colour. According to the report, this mysterious cave is southeast of the bluff. Without losing any time we wended our way in that direction. Meanwhile our guides began to remark that they heard no noise, and no pebbles or rocks were being thrown at us. This gave them such courage that they were determined to find the cave. But our search, which lasted several hours, was in vain. After travelling until dark on and around the bluff, without finding any mysterious opening or cave, we concluded that we would look for a good camping place. Next morning we would return home and report that, as we knew beforehand, the story of the nine dead men and the ten whales is an Indian yarn. Just before retiring for the night, one of the men ascended to the summit of the mountain and fired off two barrels of his gun to arouse, as he said, the ghost from his lethargy — in case he should be asleep.

We enjoyed ourselves capitally. We spent a most pleasant night around a large fire which our guides had started and which they kept going until morning. However, we suffered considerably for the want of water, as none can be found beyond midway of the mountain.

November 3. — Our descent, which we commenced at daylight, was very pleasant until we came within an hour's walk from the water's edge. Then we stood before precipices frightfully deep, which delayed our return home for several hours. We had to repeatedly return on our tracks and find other paths. At last we arrived at the spot where we had left our canoe the day before with no other mishap save that my dog, which we had taken along as a bodyguard, had fallen into one of the ravines and could not be gotten out.

We arrived at the Mission about dusk. Our Mission flag was hoisted at the stern of our canoe as a sign of victory of the Cross over pagan superstitions. Upon our landing no Indians could be seen outside of the houses. Only one man came to meet us. He was a young fellow who had backed out of his promise to accompany us the day before. Upon seeing us come home alive the first remark which he made was to the effect that now he was convinced that the belief and legends were pure invention.

November 4. — Great excitement and confusion. I had no visitors today.

November 5. — This being Sunday quite a number were at Mass. I availed myself of the opportunity to speak again against their superstitions and bring in a few items about our trip to the mountain. I finished by exhorting them to abandon their pagan beliefs.

After Mass one of the chiefs invited the tribe to his house, where speeches were made by all the most influential men, who exhorted their friends to hold on to the old faith. In proof of their being on the side of truth, they gave as proof the loss of my Newfoundland dog. The priest was not hurt because he is a bachelor and continent.

November 6. — I sent a couple of Indians to look for my dog, with the promise of a pair of blankets in case they can bring him back alive. The brute was brought home in sound condition. The Indians said little, but I noticed that their minds are not calm.

November 10. — It is reported that the leaders of the tribe are using all means in their power to keep their influence over the people. They are making speech after speech to the young men to stick to the old practices.

I am having a great time here. I noticed before now that when the Bishop appointed me to come to this coast, I was getting charge of a great parish. Their superstitions are so numerous and so absurd that they are almost incredible. Just think — they won't allow us to have any salmon for fear that I might fry it in lard, or boil it in an iron pot! I will get the better of them anyway — tomorrow I will go out fishing myself, if the weather permits.

November 11. — I asked a couple of boys to come with me and have a canoe ride on the bay. I took along a line and a spoon bait. Before speaking of my good luck, I must first state that yesterday I had sent a young man for a salmon and had paid three fish hooks for it. The owner of the salmon was out at the time, so the messenger simply told the woman in the house that he was taking one of the "sacred" fish for the priest and in due time he gave it to me. When the owner of the salmon came home, he was told that one was missing. He at once called three friends to accompany him to my house. Seeing the now-famous salmon about to pass under the knife, he sprang forward and took it away. Throwing me the three fish hooks, he went on his way growling. This upset me so much that I resolved to go out fishing myself.

As soon as I got away from the shore with my boys, I threw out a line and spoon bait. After a few minutes we caught a fine, large salmon. Upon landing, I called the dog and put the salmon into a basket, which was against the rules. The brute took the basket and preceded me home. Of course no Indian would attempt to molest the large, faithful animal. Quite a number of men and chiefs assembled in my house, and protested against my using a knife or frying pan. I took no notice, and proceeded with my work. My aim was to show them that their superstitions were absurd and to try by all and every means to get them to give them up.

November 14. — A young man, Clawish, has gone out to the inlet, a great place for salmon. He proposes to let us have some in spite of the opposition of the tribe. Toward evening a couple of young men come to the house with some salmon. I notice that the head is cut off, and the fish split open — perhaps too the fish are not fresh. I send them off with my compliments, for I have been told that the superstitious observances are only applied in the case of fresh salmon not yet beheaded or cut open.

November 20. — Clawish brings us a supply of fresh salmon. It is easy to notice the feelings of indignation of the old people. But they are afraid to do more than make a few remarks of remonstrance, owing to the presence of seven white men, who have just arrived. They propose to go prospecting in Muchalat Arm for gold, and on our peninsula for coal.

At a meeting of the tribe, the chief speakers predict famine for the rest of the winter.

November 25. — After a spell of stormy weather the sea has become calm and the Indians have gone out fishing. The salmon are abundant — hundreds of the large fish are brought to camp.

November 30. — A second meeting of the chiefs took place last night. When everyone was in bed one of the chiefs sent a messenger to awaken all the inferior chiefs and call them to his house. The great subject was discussed. Most of the men inclined to give up the superstitions and make peace with the priest.

Tom-Sick Lepieds, a famous old cripple, and a notorious thief was arrested by the local Indian policemen. He was accused and found guilty of stealing an old blanket, a piece of tobacco and one yard of Indian beads. He was condemned by the Chief Constable to pay a fine of two new blankets within one week from date. If not paid within the time mentioned, Tom is to return to the courtroom of the Mission, and submit to having his head shaved. The theft was committed during Mass on the occasion of the blessing of the church.

December 5. — I went to Barkley Sound with six men in a canoe, according to orders received from His Lordship, Bishop Seghers. I made arrangements with the Indians of that Sound for establishing a mission. The spot which I selected is Namukamis, the property of the Ohiet Indians.

Upon my arrival here early in the morning, we noticed quite a number of people sitting before the houses as is their wont. One of them got up and made a speech. My guides told me that he was insulting us and objected to our landing. They wanted no priest and could take care of themselves without the help of the white men. I have noticed in my travels that the Indians have a horror of having what they say written down. I quietly took a pocketbook and pretended to write down the gist of the savage's speech. Whereupon he stopped at once and disappeared behind one of the houses. We then quietly landed, were invited to enter the lodge of the Chief, and were kindly received by him and his family.

All the Indians assembled in the Chief's house about noon. After baptizing the newly-born, I explained the object of my visit. The Indians rejoiced at the idea of having a resident priest in their neighbourhood. The Chief told us in a neat speech that we could have all the land we required for the purpose, and we should make our own selection as to locality.

December 26. — We had midnight Mass. Nearly all the men of the tribe were present, but only very few women. At midnight Mass, which I sang myself, I preached on the mystery of the day.

December 27. — The young men, I am reliably informed are, with very few exceptions, doing the Osemitch.[22] This is a religious practice resorted to by all the Indians, and is considered to be of the greatest importance and necessity. After inquiries, I discovered that the Indians do not have all the same way of performing this religious practice. Yet they all consider it necessary as a preparation for everything of great importance, be it the hunt, the war or the like.

They address a mysterious being, one they call Haweim, who dwells over the mountains. To him they pray for whales, sea otters and bears. Kwayetsim is the favorite of the medicine men, and all the people have recourse to him for health. And they pray to We'a Kwaitliume for strength and success at war. They have also one whom they address to give them abundance of fish and he is called Wawittillsois.[23]

When the sun rises and just before it sets, young mothers pray to that orbit for a happy delivery at childbirth. One of the main rules to be observed is to go inside the house just before sundown and not to go out again for fear of harm. The moon is also prayed to. But one man told me that his uncle, who initiated him, made him pray to a being — not mentioning the name or locality of its existence — who had it in its power to give him sea otters and seals.

When they are at sea in bad or dangerous weather, they pray to a queen, Wakouix — in, above or beyond the seas. They ascribe to her the heaving or swelling of the waves. They shout out to her asking her to cause the waves to calm down.

To some Indians the Osemitch is a very severe performance. They fast four days, are up at night and dive in the sea four times each night. As they rise above the waves, they speak out in shout-like utterances asking for sea otters. Others have only two nights on the sea, and they confine themselves to swimming and praying. Others do not take to the salt water at all.

66

But bathing in fresh water is required by all and in all cases — by some, four days, others only two. However, everyone goes in turn, apart from the tribe, and the company of his friends, to pray. As a rule he goes to the woods, strips naked alongside of a stream or a clear pool of water, and then rubs his body with a kind of grass, or brushwood or roots. In many cases he leaves the marks on his body and draws blood. The number of bunches for this charm varies according to the instructions from the one by whom he has been initiated. During all the time that he rubs his body and members, he constantly repeats in short shout-like accents, a formula of prayer expressing the object he prays for. You will often find, in the neighbourhood of where the Indian goes to pray, a skeleton or bunches of charms or weeds. Often small cedar sticks are put up to represent a man with a spear in his hands aimed at a bunch of fern roots, or the like, representing a fur seal.

In his house the savage has his own charm, which he keeps sacred and uses as circumstances call for. Only in extreme cases, such as the dangerous sickness of a child, does he make a display of them. The other day, one of our Indians, either through pride or with some other object in view, perhaps the appeasing of the bad spirit who was in his sick little boy, exposed his charms before all those present in his house. The subject was very much talked about. The charms which the Indians keep concealed are the bones of dead people, also hair, nails of the hands, beaks of birds and feathers.

I know an Indian who went sealing the other day. Before he left he opened the coffin of an old woman, cut or plucked out one or both of her eyes and put them in his pocket. When he arrived at the sealing ground, he rubbed his face with them in the region of his eyes. This was done to clear them and discover the seals as they slept on the waves.

When the Indians do the Osemitch, they have recourse to a great many ways besides those mentioned above. They all amount to very much the same thing and can be ranked under the name of superstitious practices. The old people preach strict continence to the young men and none who do not live apart from their wives can expect to be successful in the pursuit of whales and fur seals. As a preparation the time limit is ten months for whales and five calendar months for fur seals. This mode of living is only to be given up when the hunting season is at an end.

In order to avert evil the Indians have recourse to different means. On the occasion of an eclipse I have known them to throw baskets of food into the sea, at the same time uttering a formula of prayer. I have, in unfavourable weather at sea, seen them throw food on the waves and then blow a whistle which they use for the Wolf festivities. After a bad dream about a child, the parents of the child paint its face red and burn a blanket, calico prints or something of the kind to appease the bad spirit or their divinity.

January 10, 1877. — About midnight we were called up by about half a dozen Hesquiat Indians, who, coming from the inlet, brought the news of Chief Nitaska's death. Nitaska, although not the head Chief of the tribe, was considered the most influential man here and was renowned all along the coast. He was a fine orator.

At the request of the messengers we rang the church bell and in a few minutes nearly all the men were at the Mission building. The excitement was immense. The shouting and the unearthly cries of the people at this unusual hour of the night frightened the women and children. Directly, speeches began to follow the first excitement. They all amounted to the same sentiment, "Nitaska is not dead, for he has children." The man is supposed to have been swamped as he passed in his canoe too close to a well known whirlpool, where several are said to have drowned.

January 11. — Nitaska's death is a great event in this region. The tribe are mourning and general gloom hangs over the village. The dead man was evidently a great favourite and very much liked. As for us, we consider his death almost a blessing for our work. The man's influence was too great and he was inclined to work against us as regards the conversion of the people.

The Indians say that his body is not in the salt water because, if it were in the sea, there would not be any herring. Today there are immense schools up the inlet.

Availing themselves of the state of mind of the Indians, three medicine women go into trances and predict the death of the second Chief. This gives his parents considerable uneasiness. I am told this is an old dodge of that class of impostors. Their object is to get presents from the relatives or parents of those whose death they predict.

January 24. — One medicine woman caused a great deal of excitement in the village this morning. She came out of the tent, her head covered with down, dancing and shaking her head as one who has fits, meanwhile spitting out mouthfuls of blood. In this state she rushed into the homes of the three first chiefs, predicting death for the sons of the families. One of the families gave her a blanket, another a bladder of whale oil, but the third, more sensible than the others, took no notice. At last she retired, to the great relief of the credulous.

January 27. — One Indian died after a few days of sickness. The cause of his death is explained as follows. His dog slept for a few days alongside his master. At daylight the dog went outside and began to howl ... A few days later the man took sick and soon died. The cause of his death is ascribed to the howling of the dog.

January 28. — Subsequent to the drowning of Nitaska, Townissim got into unexpected trouble. Nitaska was the leader of a crew who had taken the old Chief to the police in Victoria. He was a rival of the first Chief, and had been instrumental in capturing him and removing him to jail. Ever since the death of their favourite, the old people have felt very morose. Some of the most wicked have spread the news and attributed the accident to the fact that Townissim, since his return from Youil, had constantly prayed for the death of Nitaska. Hence they secretly resolved to kill him. But secrets among Indians are likely to leak out, and so it happened in this case.

The plan for killing Townissim was very simple. A day was determined, a Sunday after High Mass. A feast was announced to take place in one of the houses, and all the Indians were to be present. Whilst they would be eating, a daring old warrior was to get up without warning and stab the old Chief. This was to be a signal for others to get up and stab him to death.

Just before Mass a young Indian, a relative of the Chief, walked into my house downhearted and despondent. He told me about the events that were to take place and pleaded for my interference. I sent for the old Chief and cautioned him against going to the entertainment. I need hardly add that he strictly followed my instructions.

Next I sent for the man, Tsokwit, who was to commit the murder and put him on his guard. He did not deny his evil intentions and those of the tribe. But after a good deal of reasoning he promised that he would not commit the crime. However, the old Chief more than ever abstained from going out alone after dark. And then, whether day or night, he always carried a weapon concealed under his clothes.

March 1. — Ever since the beginning of last month, with the exception of the last three days, the Indians have been unable to go fishing. They are suffering very much from hunger. This circumstance I made use of to make the Indians understand that the idea that chiefs will send food to their relatives from the other world after their death is absurd. Nitaska was a great chief and yet sent no whale or food to his starving relatives. I am almost losing patience and use every opportunity to impress on their minds the idea that they will have to renounce their old beliefs.

March 8. — There arrived here last night four Kyuquot men on a very important errand. As they walked into our Indian room, they presented a most alarming appearance. Their faces were painted black with red circle around their eyes. Their only covering was a piece of blanket around their waist and in their hands they held Indian muskets pointed as if ready for shooting. They were followed by a number of Hesquiats, who were suspicious of evil designs on the part of the visitors and were ready for any emergency. One of the strangers, acting as spokesman, placed the butt of his gun on the floor and held it with one hand whilst with the other he made indescribable gestures. His chest began to heave and, panting for breath, he at last spoke out in a loud coarse voice. He had big news to tell. His son, a lad whom I knew well, was missing. The report had it that whilst on his way from Puget Sound to his home in Kyuquot, his canoe had capsized off one of the Nitinat villages at the entrance of the Straits. Thence, having reached shore alive, he and three of his companions had travelled on foot with the object of reaching one of the Ohiet villages near Barkley Sound. This was only a report. But the speaker, the father of the young man and a very influential man at home, was of the opinion that by this time his young son was with the Ohiet Indians. This idea seemed to have a great effect on the state of his mind. He added that if his son had been maltreated by the Nitinat Indians or killed by them, two hundred warriors of the Kyuquot tribe would go on the warpath and avenge the death of the young Chief.

The four men here now are a detachment of a crew of twenty men now camped at Vamis and detained by headwinds. They intend to walk back to the spot where they left their friends and then sail to the Nitinat coast, as soon as the weather allows.

March 20. — This day is marked by a welcome change in the condition of the natives. Since the 5th of the month, the Indians had been unable to go fishing and had very little food in their houses. They were actually starving and their little children have been crying for food. You can see the misery on the faces of both old and young. The oldest people assert that within their memory they have never been in such a state of distress. Today, the weather being fine, an abundance of herring and salmon were brought to the camp.

As regards the spiritual state of the tribe, it is worse than ever. They blame me for the absence of food. They laugh at the doctrine which I teach. I gain nothing by making the sign of the Cross. I am neither a white man nor an Indian. I am the *Chigha*, the devil.

March 25. — This day, Palm Sunday, Reverend Father Nicolaye left after Mass for Ucluelet, Barkley Sound. There he will join a schooner which is soon expected to sail to Victoria. Complaints of illness are the cause of his departure. I am under the impression that the poor Father is not really sick. He is sick at heart at the discouraging state of affairs here. Indeed our position would almost make an angel lose heart and courage. Solitude. We have not seen a white man since October and we have not received any mail for several months. Our provisions are nearly all gone and what remains is of the poorest kind. And our Indians are as bad, and as much attached to their pagan ideas as before we commenced our work here. Father Nicolaye left me. God bless the poor man and restore him to health.

March 30. — There is some rejoicing in the camp. A canoe of visitors brought the news that there was a scarcity of provisions and great deal of distress in all the villages on the coast. When our Indians meet with misfortune they always feel much relieved when they hear that others of their class have met with misfortune also. My people feel good today.

April 28. — Reverend Father Nicolaye arrived back from Victoria about midnight by canoe. He brought orders from the Bishop that I must leave at once and report to the Episcopal city, where a synod is to be held. The canoe which brought the Father took me to Clayoquot, where I found the schooner *Anna Beck*, Douglas Warren in command.

May 15. — I arrived back at the Mission today about noon. With the exception of Father Nicolaye, all the priests of the diocese were present at the synod.

May 20. — Today, Pentecost Sunday, all the Indians were at Mass, save three men and a few women. As I told them on Easter Sunday that I would call on this day for the names of those who want to be baptized, I received ninety-four men and women on the list of candidates. It is evident that the movement is too general to be worthy of confidence. All the medicine men and women offer themselves as candidates for instruction as a preparation for the sacrament of regeneration.

January 5, 1878. — I returned here yesterday from Namukamis, Barkley Sound, where I had been superintending the building of a new Mission since the 24th of last August. It will be dedicated to Almighty God, under the patronage of St. Leo the Great.

Before leaving for the Yukon River, Alaska Territory, the Bishop commissioned me to go and superintend the building of the new Mission. I left Hesquiat at the end of July, and went to Victoria to make the necessary preparations. Father Nicolaye, for whom the new mission was to be built, remained in Hesquiat.

I left Victoria on the *Favorite*, Captain Hugh McKay, on the 23rd of August, accompanied by a French-Canadian carpenter called Morrin. We arrived the next day in a small bay on Tzartus Island, opposite the Sarita River. From there we went in canoes to the selected spot for the building close to the Namukamis village.

Our first work was to put up a small cabin, 12x12. This was to be our residence for over four months. The walls were made of flooring and the floor was mother-earth. As it happened, the weather turned out to be very moist. For three months we were living as if in a cloud. It rained day and night. It soon appeared that our roof was not close, the water freely streamed through the crevices and, as the wind occasionally blew quite lively, we found that our walls were not much of a protection. Our cabin was built on a slope and the water streaming from the hill above found its way to the ocean over our uncovered floor.

My work was to look after the Indian labourers and do the cooking. We had a bunk on each side of the cabin, a stove in the middle, and a small table and a bench at the end of the room. Under the bunks we stowed our provisions — bacon, potatoes, rice and beans. The flour we kept in a small barrel as a protection from the mice which infested our odd dwelling. I made bread as often as required. The Indians we fed on biscuit and molasses. One morning, having neglected to cover the bucket in which we kept our molasses over night, I found twenty-four mice drowned in the sweet stuff. I carefully picked them out, unseen by the Indians. Afterward they continued to enjoy their molasses and biscuit as if nothing had happened. The Indians, unaccustomed to a white man's food, enjoyed their fare immensely. The carpenter also was satisfied with my culinary efforts. Altogether we had rather a pleasant time.

We squared the logs for the new building which was 64x26, twenty feet being walled off for the residence of the priest in charge. The work of the Indians consisted in cutting down the trees and cleaning off the branches. After the carpenter had finished squaring them, the Indians took them down to the site of the building. We found all the timber which we required on the spot. We even made the shingles ourselves. With the exception of the flooring and window cases, no lumber was used from the saw mills. It was slow work, yet it was pleasant to see a lot of wild men at work and to hear them from morning to night.

I said the first Mass in the new building on Christmas Day. Father Nicolaye arrived at this new residence on the New Year's Eve, so I left on the second day of the year for Hesquiat.

From the beginning of this year all the Indians of Barkley Sound, and down to Port San Juan, will be attended to from St. Leo's Mission.

Before taking charge, Reverend Father Nicolaye gave me a short account of the conduct of the Hesquiat during my five months' absence.

He continued to preach Sunday after Sunday against the Indians' superstitions, and the medicine men. He told them that none could expect to be baptized except if they would not first abandon their practices. In a moment of fervor forty men and women resolved to comply with the conditions. Before ten days had elapsed ten of the number had transgressed the rules. In a few days more, sickness having broken out in the settlement, recourse was freely had to the medicine men and women. In short, when he left for his new mission only seven had remained faithful. The old people are most determined to frustrate our plans. Two of them, Eskowit and Eagakom, have declared that they will kill the priest in case their sons die.

A young man, Nagokwit, one day entered the house and began to abuse Father Nicolaye. Next he raised his hand to strike the Father, but he was pushed back and prevented from carrying out his design by some friendly Indians who happened to be present.

January 15. — On the feast of the Epiphany very few Indians were at Hesquiat. Almost all the tribe were fishing at the head of the inlet. The weather being better last Sunday all the men came to Hesquiat to attend church. There were also quite a number of women.

The few who are preparing for baptism are young men and three young women. The old people are once more holding up their old superstitions as regards the winter salmon. There was a row on account of some of the most reasonable threatening to use their iron pots to boil the fresh salmon.

January 22. — A dead whale was found on the beach this side of Estevan Point. It was cut up by the natives who reside there at this time of year. Everyone helped himself the best way he could; almost all the chiefs and the rightful owners of a share of the big fish are absent at the inlet. These, upon hearing the news, hurried to Estevan, but found that very little is left for them. This greatly enraged them and trouble was imminent. Finally they confined themselves to going from house to house and taking away all the blubber they came across. This amounted to very little. The thieves had concealed the principal part of the booty in the bush with the expectation of fetching it home when the excitement is over.

January 25. — I am informed that most of the blubber of the famous whale is now being boiled and the oil pressed out at some distance away in the bush.

March 1. — Since the middle of January there has been a great scarcity of food. Owing to the easterly gales, which commenced last October and which have not been interrupted by fair weather except for a few days about New Year's, no one has been able to go fishing. All, without exception, are very hard up. The second Chief, a nice young fellow, came to my house today about noon. He told me in a pathetic tone that my dog had taken away a piece of whale blubber, the only food there was left. He asked me to lend him some flour so that they might have a decent meal for a day or two. The flour was given with a good heart and the poor fellow went away rejoicing. I find it very hard and painful to see the suffering of these people for want of food.

March 3. — The state of the weather is more satisfactory. The Indians avail themselves of it to go out fishing. A large amount of salmon is caught in the inlet and at Hesquiat. The superstitions are as strong as last year. The old people are desperate and most abusive against anyone who transgresses the old customs. Quite a few of the young people do not mind them.

March 11. — A young fellow was whipped by the police for running away with his uncle's wife.

March 14. — The Indians are drying salmon. This was never before done on this coast. The Indian basket is also used to carry the famous fish to the houses from the canoes.

A canoe arrives from Clayoquot and reports the Indians of those parts are in very great distress, owing to a lack of food. One of their number, the Juggler, who claims the power to make the herring flock to their harbour by incantations, finds himself disappointed, not one herring having thus far been seen in the neighbourhood. A few days ago he ordered the Indians out in their canoes, having noticed, as he thought, by the appearance of immense flocks of sea gulls, that the herring were coming in. He claimed credit for this event, but in the evening the canoes came back disappointed. His father and his nearest relatives in public speeches put the blame on one vicious young fellow who last year had crushed the head of a fresh herring with a stone.

April 13. — This beautiful weather of the last two weeks, and which will continue fine, puts an end to the destitution of the Indians. There is an abundance of salmon, codfish, halibut and rock cod.

The women had, since the beginning of the famine, through bad weather and rain, gone out to their different fern and wild clover patches to dig up roots. Now they look happy and contented as they cut up the fish, hang it up to dry in the sun and prepare it for the use of their households.

April 14. — I received this morning the intelligence of the death of

74

Pope Pius IX. — R.I.P. — and the accession to the pontifical throne of Leo XIII. The late Pope died February 7.

April 17. — There was an Indian marriage today. This is not the first or most important since I resided here. The marriages of the people are arranged by the parents of the young, at least this is the general rule. Girls who have both parents alive are preferred to orphan girls, and the daughters of chiefs or wealthy people are generally preferred to those of inferior Indians. The fact is, the Indian is essentially a speculator. The parents of the young man are in favour of a girl who has both parents because they hope that these parents will continue to support their daughter by giving her presents, clothing and other useful articles. In many cases the wish of the young man is not much considered. He is told by his parents or guardians that they are going to propose to a certain girl. As a rule he consents.

Then commences a number of secret visits to the elders. Small articles are given as presents. Good humour and kindness are all had recourse to. At last the parents of the would-be benedict invite the girl's parents and nearest relatives to a sumptuous meal. If the secret has leaked out, they almost invariably decline the invitation. The food is then carried to their houses. Sometimes it is returned, in which case the girl is to be refused and no union is to take place. In other cases it is partaken of, but yet the news reaches the parents of the boy that their plans are to be frustrated. So another article, generally food, is returned to make up for that already consumed. If the invitation is accepted or the food distributed to the nearest relatives, it is a sign that there will be a marriage.

Shortly after the preparatory step, two or three important men go, still on the sly, and make more open proposals. If no answer is given it is a good and favourable sign. Without delay quite a crowd of the most important men approach the girl's parents and speak plain and open language that everybody must listen to. It consists of first extolling the dignity and importance of the relatives of the future bride. Then they give a word of recommendation in the same vein to the bridegroom.

Sometimes an answer is given, but as often the speakers are quietly told to return to their houses. This means that the matter is settled. The girl very often is not consulted, but it is almost sure that she will not live with the young man except if she feels like it. Threats, entreaties and all kinds of means will have no effect in many cases on young girls when they have made up their mind to marry somebody else. Yet the marriage ceremony must take place if the parents have not positively refused their assent to the union.

The ceremony commences by a crowd of people gathering on the beach and walking in the direction of the house of the girl's parents. They advance to the measure of the tambourine, the women covered with feathers and their faces painted. They all sing some of their old songs. Now and then one or more of the women raise their voices above all the surrounding *vacarme* and unearthly noise. Occasionally they stand for a moment on their heels and swing their bodies about, at the same time stretching out their arms, over which hang their coloured blankets. Then they proceed to their destination. To the looker-on, from a distance, it presents a savage yet attractive scene.

At last they all stop before the bride's residence, or the house where the union is to be declared and contracted. One of the important men acts as orator. For hours and hours he stands at the head of the crowd, his face turned towards the residence of the girl's parents. He talks and talks, mentioning the reasons why and how, the noble deeds of the forefathers and the importance of the clan. Call it flattery? Why, in most cases it is rank untruth. But, never mind, his object is to please. I have seen them and heard them for two and three days, talking all the while before a house, whether there was anyone in it or not. To a civilized being, it is the greatest entertainment possible.

While this is going on, one of the men, from time to time, walks up to the door of the house and places two or more blankets before it. There is then a discussion, and again more blankets are presented. The nearest relatives are included in the recipients of presents. At last it all finishes by the word being passed that the girl is given to the boy and a stop is put to the ceremonies.

The age at which Indians marry varies, but it is an unusual case when a young woman is not married before she is sixteen. Many of them are joined in wedlock at thirteen and fourteen. The young men now marry when they are about sixteen or seventeen. But I am told that in the past it was the custom to postpone looking for a wife for a young man who was below twenty or twenty-two.

As said above, the girls are not openly consulted in matrimonial matters. Their mothers, or aunts or other near relatives are generally informed privately. They do a great deal of persuading or dissuading of the future bride. When the contracting ceremonies are over, it soon leaks out whether the girl will consent to live with her husband. If not, you will see on the face of the latter fingernail scratches, or on his back a torn shirt, or other marks or expressions that his new life is a hard one. In an attempt to make love to her he has met with resistance and even hard treatment. This sometimes lasts for weeks, and then, after a worse scene than ever, the young man packs up and returns to his own home.

It is unusual to have a union broken off so peremptorily. In most cases it is only a bluff. Indians are very touchy, and in matrimonial cases they are very much determined that their friends shall not find an occasion to jeer at them. So then, after a time, new advances are made and a number of the most intimate friends of the discarded husband go in body to the parents of the girl. There they make more speeches and especially more presents to the relatives of the girl. In all likelihood a favourable answer will be given again. And so it goes on until the girl finally consents or gives unmistakable signs that she forever repudiates the idea of becoming the wife of the young man.

The Wedding Feasts. When a favourable answer has been obtained, the father or guardian of the young man sends a number of presents, especially articles of food, to the parents of his new daughter-in-law. Without much delay, the tribe is invited to a feast, at the end of which it is announced to all present that the occasion of the feast is the marriage of his daughter. Meanwhile, the young wife has been entertained at a choice meal by her new parents-in-law. These, in their turn, a day or two later, take their daughter to her new home and deliver her over to her husband. At the same time they make suitable presents of food, which are also partaken of by the whole tribe. Compliments are passed during the meal, and general rejoicings are engaged in. In the evening especially, the Indians assemble in the house where the young people reside, and sing and dance, and have a general good time.

It is always understood that in case no offspring be born to the newly-married couple it will be in order for the young man to separate from his wife and contract a new alliance. This is also the case where children are born, but die soon after birth. All Indians, without distinction, want an heir. The old people especially will discard a daughter-in-law who is not the mother of at least one grandchild.

June 18. — There was one peculiarity about the marriage which took place yesterday. The young man for whom the ceremonies were gone through was absent in Nootka Sound during the performance. He knew only upon landing that he was now a married man.

When marriages are contracted between parties of different tribes the ceremonies are about the same, save that the strangers come in their canoes, which they ornament with a symbol of some kind having reference to old-time ideas, legends or important facts.

A singular case came to my notice with reference to a marriage of two parties of different tribes. They were already married two days and the

77

man had not yet spoken to his wife. In fact, he did not know to which girl he was married.

July 29. — Having made a trip to Victoria where I arrived June 20, Feast of Corpus Christi, I have just returned and am sorry to learn that during my absence the greatest disorder has reigned. Some of the young men who, as I thought, were preparing for baptism were among the leaders.

September 1. — I have just made a trip to the Checkleset, and Way [24] tribes — the Kyuquots, the largest Indian settlement on the coast, were absent at Quatsino. I saw only a few of them and was informed that the tribe is very orderly. The people are very anxious to have a resident priest.

September 15. — I went to Barkley Sound and saw Father Nicolaye at Namukamis. He seems to be making good headway amongst the Ohiet.

With regard to the Hesquiats, I must say that there is now not one Indian left, man or woman, who has remained faithful to the conditions laid down as a preparation to baptism. Some have altogether returned to their superstitious practices, whereas the others are very unruly in different other ways.

October 6. — A dead whale is found on the beach at Hole in the Wall. The Indians belonging to the outside camp bring the news to Hesquiat. The finding of a dead whale is always an occasion of great disturbance and trouble. This one is not an exception. A man called Manakoah, in protecting his piece, received a bad cut on the arm from a young man called Nayokwit.

November 7. — From all accounts I am gaining in the esteem of the Indians. In their meetings my name is seldom mentioned with the angry feelings that it was last year. The motive may be that they have experienced that transgressing their old rules does not affect their success at fishing. The young men, however, are as usual addicted as ever to the *Osemitch.* You can read it in their countenance, the skin having been rubbed off by the use of their charms.

November 16. — There was a severe thunder-storm today. There is now a light seen in the direction of the inlet. It is so similar to the light of a vessel that most of the Indians take it to be the light of some vessel in distress. A canoe went out, but was driven back by the storm.

November 17. — The light of yesterday turns out to be the light of a bush fire caused by lightning. This is taken as a proof that thunder is not a bird, as birds do not make fires.

There was quite a discussion in my house about the thunder yesterday. The Indians maintain that it is an immense bird — the

Thunderbird. One of the young men told me that Koninah, the third Chief, was in possession of one of its wing feathers. I sent for the feather, but the young fellow came back disappointed. Koninah stated that he had not such feather. The noise of the thunder is explained by the fact that the Thunderbird takes hold of a whale and in a struggle with the monster causes all the thundering reports.

The lightning is a reflection of the bird's eyes which it opens and closes in rapid succession. Others have it that the neck of the bird is surrounded by a being, Heitlik, of the shape of a snake. [25] Heitlik breaks loose and in flames goes about scattering what we call lightning. Others again say that the light comes from under the wings of the bird which becomes visible as the bird flaps its wings.

January 26, 1879. — Archbishop Seghers arrived here very unexpectedly a few days ago. He brought news that he is to go to Oregon as coadjutor *cum jure successioris* of Archbishop Blanchet.

Upon arriving, the Archbishop told me that he had come to baptize my Indians. I replied that none were fit to receive the sacrament. He insisted. In order to avoid all further controversies I confined myself to the cooking. After a couple of days he commenced to see that it was premature to speak of baptism to most of the people. He thought, however, that it was wrong to be over-exacting, both as to knowledge and conduct. Today ten people, six men and four women, received the sacrament of regeneration at the hands of the new Archbishop of Oregon. All the Indians were present and the long ceremonies of the Ritual were followed.

January 27. — Archbishop Seghers left Hesquiat in a canoe. I accompanied him.

February 9. — We stopped a full day in Ahousat, where we assembled all the Indians in the Chief's house. As usual they were very noisy but very friendly. We passed the other tribes, going directly to Namukamis where we met Father Nicolaye. On Sunday the Bishop blessed the new church of St. Leo. The weather was very stormy and most of the Indians who were living on Tzartus Island were unable to come across. Quite a few of the men were present.

I arrived home with my Indians having left the Bishop, who is on his way to Victoria, in the house of Father Nicolaye.

I have just returned from Victoria where I have made my usual purchases for the next twelve months. Nothing unusual has occurred these last three or four months. Upon my return home I learned that several of the Indians baptized by the Archbishop have returned again to the pagan practices — only three or four have remained faithful. As I had foreseen this, it did not upset me much. In fact I had told his Grace that such would be the case. As the Indians also mistrusted these would-be Christians it caused very little scandal.

They are now, however, watching with some concern the conduct of one who is supposed to be sincere about his Christianity. The fact is his wife has just given birth to a little boy. Everyone watches the couple to see whether they will not have recourse to the Indian medicine man or woman. Never within the memory of even the oldest people was a child born and not at once taken charge of by one or more sorcerers. The children of the chiefs and important people are especially subject to the treatment of those imposters.

As soon as a child is born, one or more are invited, or invite themselves, to handle the poor little creature. A woman who expects to become a mother soon will be sure to live in the neighbourhood of the medicine woman, or at least, she will move to where she can have easy access to them. Up to now the Indians were under the impression that a child cannot live except if it be doctored Indian fashion. There is no word to express how they will humble themselves and how slavish they will become in order to secure the services of the savage doctor. If a young man is the son of a medicine man or medicine woman his chances for marriage are far superior to those who have no such dignitaries in their immediate household. The Indians told me that to become Christians, they could give up everything, but their doctors.

The services of these imposters are called for and made use of at all times. Upon the birth of an infant several of them rush to the place. They all take hold of the newly-born, sing, squeeze its little belly, pretend to cast out the evil one and often exhaust the little one to death.

July 21. — The father of the child is a determined, good man. He has an amount of trouble with his relatives who all want him to take the child to the doctors. The infant is weak and gives doubtful signs of a long existence. This gives them a chance to find fault with him all the more. But he does not mind their suggestions or interference. In my own mind, I can see the consequences if the infant should die. Never again would an Indian listen to us under similar circumstances. Indians are exceedingly fond of having an heir and are passionately attached to their offspring. I make daily visits to the newcomer, but he is not a great success. He cries a great deal and the people all say that it is because the evil one was not cast out by the sorcerers.

August 28. — I just returned from Kyuquot and other tribes. My instructions from Archbishop Seghers were to feel the pulse of the Kyuquots with regard to having a priest stationed at that place. Part of the tribe had moved to their river stations, but the Chief and several of the most important men were still at Aktese, their summer residence. The Chief not only told me that he was anxious to have a resident priest, but he promised to grant all the land required for the use of the missionary, free of charge. Other important men also spoke and expressed their happiness at the idea of having a chance to have their children properly educated.

My opinion of the Kyuquots is that it will be hard to manage the old people. As regards the boys and girls, of whom there are hundreds, I consider it to be the very finest Mission. Not only on the island, but in the diocese.

December 3. — The greatest obstacle to the conversion of the Indians is the idea that they will have to give up the sorcerers. I know a young woman who refused to marry a young man because he intended to become a Christian. The idea that he would object to her consulting the doctors, both for herself and their children, made her reject his advances of matrimony.

The sorcerer is either a man or a woman on this coast. Very few men are sorcerers, but the number of women doctors is very large. In some

Grave monument of Chief Mokwinna, Friendly Cove, Nootka.

tribes three-fourths of the women and in others one-half or a third — nearly all the old women — claim some special talent in that line.

The sorcerer does not deal in drugs nor use medicine for his patients. Nor does he study medicine. He is usually put up to become a sorcerer by some relation in the craft or sometimes through motives of his own.

The starting point is either a dream or a so-called vision, or a discovery of something unusual in his wanderings on the beach. Then he will feign sickness and he retires to his couch. His friends pretend to be or are really alarmed ... He suddenly utters deep sighs or groans, does so repeatedly; then he jumps up, shaking his head, eyes closed, and intones a song supposedly taught to him by the mysterious being who inspired him to become a sorcerer.

This is the announcement to the tribe that they have a new sorcerer. The cases may differ in some of the details, but they all amount to the same. We have one here just now, the first since I have been stationed here. He is a young, sickly fellow of a silent, morose disposition. He is the last person that I would have suspected of being inclined this way. He is always sick and very likely he is trying this dodge to get well. The Indians say that when anybody is an invalid he will recover at once by becoming a sorcerer.

The Indians have been talking a good deal of their new doctor. They say that he pulled a snake out of his abdomen and that he will walk on the salt water as if it were *terra firma*. They also say that he walks on the branches of trees to their extremity, and thus passes from one tree to another. As I always strive to draw good out of evil, so I tried to in the present case. Nothing like facing the enemy. It may be hard at first, but it is the only way to convince for the future.

So I defied the hero. And on Sunday I told them what I thought of such impostors and of those who take their part. Next Sunday, November 9, about four in the morning I was aroused from my slumber by the loud voices of Indians and the noise made by their new sorcerer. He was on the top of a tree and at times barked like a dog or croaked like a raven. Then he would strike up a song or work his rattles to attract the attention of the stupefied savages.

At Mass, Michel, the head of the only family now faithful to their baptismal promises, came to see me in a despondent mood. I think I felt as bad as he did, but I composed myself and sang High Mass and preached the Gospel of the day.

At noon all the Indians of the tribe were entertained by an old couple and during the repast they were unanimous in rejoicing at the fact of having a new medicine man. The old people especially were jubilant and availed themselves of the opportunity to recommend their old superstitions to the rising generation.

I may here say that speculation was at the bottom of this general endorsement. For this, his first appearance, was the announcement that four days later he would make a gift-feast to the tribe and those who praised him most expected to be the most favoured in his acts of generosity.

When the repast was coming to an end the father of the new hero went into the house and invited all those present to follow him behind one of the houses, where his son would give proofs of his extraordinary powers.

Michel was called out by name. Like a man he got up and all the people followed him outside, expecting to see him covered with confusion. He put his hand to his mouth and as he walked at the head of the crowd, he prayed "that truth might triumph." We found the new medicine man standing at the foot of the tree on which he had been doing his performances since the early morning. All the people arrived on the spot and stood around in a circle, none daring to approach the awe-inspiring juggler. Michel, being called upon to do so, went up to him. He at once saw the preparations that had been made and showed them to all those present. Consequently, the initial step of the would-have supernatural powers was an utter failure. The trick consisted, or was supposed to consist, in the fact that the sorcerer was, by incantations, to cause the lower branches of the tree, under which he stood, to bow down. Thus by taking hold of them he could climb up the tree to the spot where he had caused the admiration of everybody in the early morning. Michel, being close by, noticed, hanging from the lower branches, a thin string which was not supposed to be there. Thus the trick fell through. One would think that the people on noticing that they were imposed upon would walk away disgusted. But not at all, their boasting changed into anger and was followed by most unusual excitement.

Three days later the medicine man made a gift-feast to the whole tribe. When all the people were assembled he recommenced his wonderful performances. Once more Michel was called upon. He was equal to the occasion, and before long he was advised by a thoughtful friend to retire, leaving the whole assembly covered with confusion. The feast went on and I was glad to learn that my friend came in for many valuable gifts.

I have been asked, "Are there real sorcerers to be found amongst your people?" My answer is, if there are any, I have never met or discovered them.

January 27, 1880. — Very extraordinary news. I received word that we have a new Bishop. I received a letter dated October from Victoria in the handwriting of Father Brondel, late of Steilacoom, Washington Territory, inviting me to go to his Consecration. It was to take place in the Cathedral of Victoria, on the 14th of December of last year.

February 25. — An Indian arrived at the Mission from Barkley Sound and delivered a letter, with a portrait enclosed, of the new Bishop of Vancouver, the Right Reverend J.B. Brondel, D.D. The new prelate expressed his astonishment that I was not present at the great celebration. A great many events take place and great celebrations in the Church are had, but, although I would be happy to be present and witness them, I must forego the pleasure owing to the lack of communication. Our new Bishop will after a time understand the situation.

April 20. — I have just returned from Victoria, where I went to pay my respects to Reverend Brondel, our new Bishop.

This visit was occasioned by a very disagreeable circumstance. Early in March the Indians became very dissatisfied and troublesome. The old people were finding fault and exciting the others at every chance. They now made up their minds that they would work on Sundays and ignore the established rules. First, they came to ask permission to go out fishing. As they pleaded scarcity of provisions, the weather having been very bad, I allowed them to go out on one Sunday, and again on the following. On the third Sunday, there being an abundance of food in the village, they went out without leave. When the bell was rung for High Mass, they all came on shore and attended Mass. I warned them and insinuated that the transgressors of our Sunday law would be punished. I could not punish them all, but the one who started the others would be the sufferer. After Mass a messenger came to tell me that all the men of the tribe were preparing to pull out their canoes.

Upon looking out I saw about thirty canoes in a line and on a certain signal being given, they all pulled out together. This was very clever on their part. I could not punish any single starter. However, I walked down to the beach and noticed that not only the men but even most of the women were bent on desecrating the Sunday. Only two or three of the Indian policemen had remained faithful. With their assistance I took away a number of nets, said a few words to the leaders, and walked back to the Mission. On my way a scuffle took place between the police and some of the worst of the lot. This I stopped without delay and without any harm being done save the tearing of a few shirts and the pulling out of a handful or two of hair.

When I got home I tried to take the matter coolly. But how could I? Here it was now nearly six years. And only one convert and two or three decent fellows, although heathens. The Apostles fared still worse, and the missionaries in China and elsewhere have no better times. Nothing like persevering and fighting the matter through.

Now, the thought struck me to leave the place for a few Sundays. What could I do if the same trouble arose again next Sunday? I was half victorious, as quite a few nets were in my possession. I therefore resolved to make a trip to Victoria to see our new Bishop. His wise counsels and a talk with my fellow priests there would give me new courage and light.

I secured a crew of six Indians and, as usual, we travelled in a canoe. The weather looked fine, but at this time of the year the nights are very cool, when one must sleep outside or in the bottom of a canoe. Yet we could expect nothing else, for the next four or five nights we could be compelled to do so. When we came within sixty miles of Victoria the weather was bitter cold, but the sea, comparatively speaking, smooth. On the shore there was considerable surf, and the northerly wind was very strong. I was so crippled up with cold that I refused to go on shore, and preferred to pass the rest of the night in the bottom of the canoe. One of my guides, hearing that my feet were actually freezing, turned about in the canoe and put the soles of his feet to those of mine. This had the desired effect and made me feel more comfortable, for the feet of the Indians are always warm, even when they walk barefoot through the snow.

I was aroused very early by the crowing of a rooster in the bush, and later on I was amused to see one of my men, in his shirt tails, running after the lonely rooster. At last he caught it and mercilessly killed it. The bird had been left there by Indians of the neighbourhood, who had, I suppose, stolen him from some farmer. We cleaned the rooster and ate him for breakfast.

I remained in Victoria three days with the new Bishop. During that time the weather had changed, and on our way back to the coast we had a favourable leading wind.

When we had made a little over a hundred miles, which we had done in less than three days and two nights, we came very near to being drowned during a severe storm. Both the Indians and myself had given up. The waves were immense and, rising like mountains, threatened to engulf us at any moment. We all lay flat in the canoe, save the man in the stern. At times our frail skiff stood almost perpendicular. At last we got on shore, soaked with the brine of the sea. We camped on a small island, where we found a good supply of driftwood. There we passed the night under *la belle étoile* and as I lay under my blankets I wondered at the myriads of stars and admired the wonderful works of God. After saying *Benedicte Stellae Coeli Domino*, I managed to take some very much needed rest.

Three days later we arrived at Hesquiat, where the Indians were becoming uneasy on account of our prolonged absence. The trouble they had given me before leaving seemed to have weighed heavily on their minds. I was reliably informed that they were determined to avoid listening to the evil counsels of their wicked leaders who, without exception, are all old men and old women.

July 28. — Right Reverend J.B. Brondel made his first episcopal visit to the coast, and, I am sorry to say, I could not report *omnia prospera*. The Bishop seemed disappointed; he expected to receive a great reception and he would have been received with all the honours due to his rank. But my Indians, with the exception of one family are still pagans. I thought it would look like hypocrisy to make them turn out and act as Christians. I live in hope that the time may yet come when our Bishop will be duly received here by Christians.

July. — The Bishop called here on his way back from further along the coast. He was accompanied by Father Nicolaye.

September 25. — These Indians are extraordinary people. There is an elderly man who of late has been giving a good deal of trouble to some of his old enemies. Several of them have come for protection and seem to be really alarmed. At the bottom of all the mischief is an old threadworn blanket.

The Indian in question is a very troublesome individual. He has the name of having been a daring warrior and at home he has had many a quarrel and fight with the people of the tribe. At last he got tired of black eyes and bruised limbs. Early one morning he came back from a long walk on the shore. He wore as usual an old blanket, his only covering. The man was frothing at the mouth and his blanket was dripping wet, apparently with blood. He called his friends together and with a trembling, hoarse voice told them that at a short distance from the settlement he had come upon a strange object. It was at the foot of a large tree and was bleeding profusely. Something seemed to tell him to take off his blanket and steep it in the red liquid. Impulsively he did so and left the spot assured that he had now in his possession a "charm", that would render him invulnerable. It would defy his enemies, whether at home or abroad.

I had often heard the Indians speak of this blanket. It was said that the wickedness of the children of this man was to be ascribed to the fact that their father, immediately after their birth, had rolled the blanket around their tiny limbs and body, while besmearing them with the juices extracted from his "charms". Not only that, the blanket had such mysterious qualities that it would be impossible to send a shot through it.

There was now quite an excitement in the tribe about the blanket. In order to destroy any further belief in the obnoxious article, I sent the men who had a new grievance against the old fellow to tell him to come over to the Mission to see me. He came, but did not bring along the mysterious covering. I had my gun in my hands and quietly told the poor fellow to go and get it. I wanted to be convinced, and that if I could not pierce a hole through it with my gun, the Indians would be justified in looking upon it with awe and dread. There were now quite a number of people around to be witnesses. Of course it all ended in confusion on the part of the old man. The others after some discussion returned to their homes convinced that they had all along been imposed upon. It is slow work, but one after another the dark spots in the Indians' minds are being cleared. A few more proofs of this kind will go a long way to make them look upon the old yarns with misgivings. Then truth at last will prevail.

There is general feasting going on just now. The festivities are called *Klookwana*.[26] They remind one of the feasts of the Mardi Gras of Europe, and from time to time are indulged in by the tribes, especially during the winter season. The origin and the spirit of this feast are, I think, the same, although the some of the details differ, in the several tribes of the west coast of the Island.

A chief or one of the leading men has prepared for the occasion. He must have a large supply of food and blankets, for he is expected to feed the tribe during the festivities. He closes the event by making a gift to everyone who has been invited and taken part. These gifts consist of canoes, blankets, axes, fruit, calico and Indian beads.

The opening ceremonies are a banquet at which all the Indians are supposed to be present. One or more of them go outside and return immediately into the house and cause consternation in the assembly by reporting that a pack of wolves are to be seen at a short distance from the camp. The wolves are some of the young men running on all fours, imitating the step of wolves. And with a tail and ears, they fairly resemble the much-to-be-dreaded animal. This is the signal for great excitement. The chiefs make speeches, the old warriors sound the alarm, songs are indulged in and fright is cast into the bosoms of old and young. And general notice is given, especially to the children, to be on their guard. On this and the next four days no work is to be done, and general rejoicing is indulged in. Banquets are given, and there is singing, dancing and joking. All kinds of drolleries are the order of the day.

This is, however, interrupted by the appearance of wolves in the morning and towards evening. They are very bold. They make for some of the children, singled out before the time of the festivities and now purposely exposed to the danger, and take them away with them in the bush. The men of the tribe, seeing this, run into their houses, take up their guns and shoot them off as they run in pursuit. You can now hear the shouts of alarm of the mothers and old women. After a while the excitement subsides and the general rejoicing recommences.

And thus the game continues for four days. Meanwhile the children that were taken away by the wolves are kept out of sight. The mothers weep, the fathers are wild with grief. Everything is done to make the uninitiated believe that real wolves have devoured their children.

It is a matter of pride for a chief and for all the tribe to have the *Klookwana* take place. No more important news can be communicated to a neighbouring settlement. It travels all along the coast and compliments are extended to all and to every friendly settlement.

In old times and even now on the coast there are tribes where ceremonies ended in mutilation, or at least wounding. But the wounding is received voluntarily and payment is made at the conclusion of the festivities. The occasion is suggested by the individual himself. He knows that as long as the *Klookwana* is on, a man who fights or quarrels with his wife or strikes her is liable to have a spear passed through the skin of his arm. This individual, I say, will purposely transgress this rule, whereupon a number of men enter his lodge, take hold of him and pass a sharp piece of iron or spear through the skin of his arm. This naturally causes fright and consternation in the women and children.

Being aware of this, I cautioned the people against doing anything of the kind, but I can see nothing to find fault with at the present time. When I see the masquerades, cavalcades, historic processions, dramas, and other entertainments of our white populations abandoned and given up forever, it will be time enough to tell the Indians that they must give up their festivities.

On the fifth day, if it is fair, the Indians all dress up. The initiated know what is to take place. The wolves, as usual, come out of the bush. This time the children, whom they had stolen, accompany them. The people get excited. They pull down to the beach two large canoes, cover them with planks and the chiefs and men and women of a special rank, using this as a platform, slowly proceed over the water to within a close distance where the supposed wolves have charge of the children. They beat the drums, dance as they proceed, sing incantation songs, fire off their guns, and at a determined moment rescue the captive children and send the defeated wolves back into the bush.

The young people are now naked, their only covering being small branches of trees and brushwood. They are solemnly, amidst songs and general rejoicing, taken to the house of the Chief, who gives the entertainment. The day is passed without any interruption in this house. The children tell of their experiences in the home of the wolves and mention the new names that they are to take. Many other ceremonies, too long and too numerous to mention, are gone through.

The feast continues at this place nearly a month. In other tribes it lasts only a week. It comes to a conclusion by the burning of the branch-covering of the children; and finally gifts are presented by the Chief who organized the festival.

July, 1881. — I have just returned from Ahousat, where I built a small church with two rooms attached for use as a house and sacristy.

To build a wooden church with the material I had at my disposition would puzzle many an architect. I had explained my plans to the Bishop, who sent me enough flooring and planks for the body of the building. Then I made the Indians get cedar, which we squared and used for sills, rafters and other necessary supports. Lastly I enlisted the services of an old fellow to bring me a supply of cedar blocks, cut in two foot lengths, which I used to make shingles. Outside, the building is neat, but the inside has the appearance of a common barn. I put up an altar and communion railing. But for the generous assistance of the natives I could never have finished the work by myself.

I have been complimented on my work. But people cannot throw dust in my eyes — it is altogether a poor job. Yet it will answer a useful purpose and has cost the best of only a few dollars.

I consider this place very necessary if I want to instruct the Indians of this tribe. This far I had done it in the house of the Chief. It was a terrible place.

This house is over one hundred feet in length by sixty in width. The corner posts are immense pieces of cedar twenty feet high. They are met on top by long sticks three feet through. One monster beam is laid across the centre and serves as a crosspiece to support the roof planks. With a fall of only about two feet, the roof looks almost flat. This is now the form of all the houses on the coast. The sides are cedar planks fastened by ropes of cedar bark below and above. The roof planks are chiseled out so as to leave a groove for the rain. In fine weather one of these planks is raised to let in air and give a place for the smoke to exit.

In the Chief's house twelve different families had their home — twelve different open fireplaces supplied the room with smoke and heat. There were no windows in the house, although the crevices between the wall planks permitted some light to enter. How could I instruct these people in such a horrible place of filth and smoke? Not to mention the noise made by the quarrelling of the women, the crying of children and the fighting dogs — and then the immodest bearing of the numerous inmates! Yes, I required a place to try and do something for the Ahousahts. Now I rejoice that when I go there next season I will have a place of my own, no matter how poor and how undesirable it may look.

During my stay I was greatly amused to see a couple of young people taking their daily walk around the place each with a shoe on one foot only. The man wore a shirt with a blanket over his shoulders and the wife had also a blanket over her dress. Both had their faces painted with red vermillion. I was told that the reason for this odd action was that they had recently become the parents of twins. By this time they had gone through a very hard experience and they were still looked upon by everyone as outcasts to be shunned. No one will use the vessels they have used either to drink or eat. Their diet is to be strictly dry fish; nothing fresh is to pass their lips. Now, and for a long time to come, they are not allowed to go on the sea in canoes either to fish or for pleasure. The man has to retire daily in the forest and by shouting and bathing reconcile the spirits. Their life is not a pleasant one as everyone avoids them. Being forbidden to work or to go out after food, they have before them the prospect of famine and endless misery. The birth of twins is a source of great excitement. They have special songs for the occasion in which all the principal men join before the house where the twins were born.

Unusual excitement was also caused by one of the chiefs going crazy. The Indians soon remembered an old remedy. They took the crazy man out to his waist in the sea. The half dozen men in charge of him carried in their hands branches of brushwood; upon a given signal, they began to flog him. Then they took the man by the hair and forced his head under water. The bubbles indicated when to allow him up for breath. Then flogging recommenced ... and his head under water again. The process was continued until very little life was left in him.

March 29, 1882. — A young Indian most unexpectedly called at my house, a few days ago, and asked to be married in the church. This was quite a new thing. Never before had anybody applied to me for matrimonial services. After mature consideration I made up my mind to comply with the man's request. And so we were at last going to have a Christian marriage. It was to be the first since I have been on the coast. The young man had not been baptized, but he was well instructed and a faithful attendant at the church and a real good fellow. He also told me that the young woman whom he was to lead to the altar was willing and anxious that I should marry them.

Indian women are never supposed to say or acknowledge that they are willing to marry a certain man. Such language is considered imprudent and immodest, so I had some difficulty in making her tell me that she wanted to marry the young man. I proceeded to marry the pair on March 23.

First I administered baptism. Then I brought them to the altar and everything went on well until I told them to join hands. This was almost too much. Single women are never to touch a young man's hand—it is an act of immodesty—and how could she do so in *conspectu omnium*, for quite a crowd were in the church? After some coaxing and persuasion, she at last put out the tip of her finger from under her blanket. The bridegroom, now rejoicing in the Christian name of John, grasped hold of it and the ceremony proceeded without any further difficulties.

I may here add that John stood before me in shirt tails, a blanket over his shoulders and barefooted. Paulina, his young bride, also wore a blanket over her dress of brown calico, and she was barefooted and bareheaded.

But the trouble, not quite unforeseen, soon arose. This Christian marriage was an innovation in these parts. The chiefs used to be consulted in these matters and did a great deal of interfering. It was often an occasion for them to be praised and rewarded for their services. Now they were ignored. The parents of the young woman refused to recognize the union. Although their consent had been asked secretly by their daughter, they had refused to accept the presents which were sent by the parents of the husband. There was such a row and such an excitement in the camp that the couple, after signing the register, refused to go to their home.

I now learned what was being said and the protestations that were uttered in public against my taking in hand their matrimonial affairs. It

Sealing schooners in Victoria Harbour, ca. 1880. *Maritime Museum of B.C. photo.*

was no business of the priest. The young people whom he wanted to marry were not his children. Such and other remarks were made by the old people, and none of their daughters would submit to such unheard-of arrangements. The idea of anyone being married in a church!

The following Sunday I preached on matrimony, explaining its sacredness. Next, I called their attention to the fact that their old marriages almost amounted to selling their daughters as one would sell a canoe or a horse—just as of old the chiefs sold their slaves. This I had told them more than once, but it had no effect. However, I knew that the young men were favourable to the Christian marriage. As they occupied one side of the church, all the women occupying seats on the other, I turned to the men. I told them to stand by me, that I would have all those who were yet single married in the church. If the girls did not comply, I would take the matter up and go with the men to look for wives in other tribes. This seems to have had the desired effect. Several women, about to be married, fearing that they would be jilted, sent word through their parents that they were not of the number who had objected to the Christian marriage.

The Indians are now preparing for the fur-sealing season. Up to a couple of years ago they lived almost exclusively on fish and potatoes. They availed themselves of the presence of large schools of dog-fish to make oil, which they sold to coasting schooners. The old people who did most of the work objected to the buying of clothing, but the young people, especially the women, did not listen to the pleadings of their elders. And they invested most of their earnings in the purchase of decent wearing apparel.

I have made it a rule that no men may come to my house unless they wear pants.

This was hard on them. They had always considered this covering of their lower limbs superfluous—a real bother. But I was inexorable. Pants on or remain outside. The other day the young Chief, a boy about ten, came to see me on business with his aunt. I saw him coming in his shirttails and a blanket on his shoulders. He had a small bundle under his arm. When within a few steps of the door he sat down on a piece of driftwood, took the parcel and shook it open. It proved to be his pants. He now put them on and solemnly walked into the Indian parlour of my house. I watched him as he left, and was amused to see him strip off the trousers, and hand them over to his aunt. Then he joined a lot of other boys in one of their favourite games.

Two years ago I persuaded the young men to try their luck as fur seal hunters. From the beginning their success was such that they now seem determined to prosecute this lucrative work and leave the dog-fish business to the old people. However, the work is not beneficial to spiritual matters. They are convinced that they must resort to the *Osemitch* for good luck. There is no use arguing with them. It is most discouraging to hear their replies and to see the determination of both men and women.

It is worth mentioning that when the young men are out sealing, the people at home observe strict old-fashioned rules. For instance, the doors of the houses must remain closed and the room be kept as dark as possible. Dogs, chickens and even children are turned outside. I heard a young man say that he missed and attributed his ill luck to the fact that at that very time a band of dogs had a row in his house, as he was afterwards informed by the women. The men go out after the seals in their canoes and, finding a seal asleep, stealthily approach and throw out their harpoon, loosely attached to a pole ten or fifteen feet long. They pull the struggling animal alongside, and kill it with a club. Guns are not used by the people when hunting the fur seal.

Another source of revenue is the sea otter, which is now scarce on the coast. They caught a few last year and the year before, altogether about seventeen, and were paid from thirty to ninety dollars in trade for each animal.

The sea otters are close in shore, rarely more than two miles away from the rocks or surf. The mode of hunting is different from that of the fur seal. Ten or twelve canoes go out together—the weather must be calm, no wind and no waves—the sea being like a looking glass, and the Indians spread themselves over an extended area. When noticing an otter, a signal is given with the paddle; then all the hunters close around the animal. The Indians use small canoes, three persons in each canoe and they use bows and arrows. The otter, on seeing danger, dives, but he must come up for breath after a while. Then the Indians begin unmercifully to shoot their arrows at him. If not hit, he dives again. When he comes up the third time he remains on the surface and, like a duck, flutters from danger the best way he can.

The Indians, having now gathered together, manage to hit and kill him amidst the greatest excitement. The man who first wounded the animal claims it as his own, although another may have done the real killing. The woman, little boy or old man who does the steering gets the tail for his share. The one who kills a wounded otter is also paid according to an agreement. And everyone who succeeded in wounding the animal is also paid, receiving one, two or more blankets as per agreement before the hunt was started.

The otter is very easily killed, a slight wound often causing death. It is sometimes very touching to listen to the narrative of the Indians on their return home from a hunting expedition. When a female otter feeds she leaves her pup floundering on the water. Otherwise she carries it always in one of her flippers. This poor brute is so attached to her offspring that she will be wounded two and three times and not part with it. She wants to protect it as long as life is in her motherly bosom. In many cases the Indians take the pup from the flippers of its lifeless mother. At other times, whilst the mother is feeding underwater, they manage to catch the helpless youngster and attach it to a rope tied in their canoe. Its wails attract the mother who, on coming in proximity of the canoe, is killed by the cunning hunter.

October 20. — On the tenth of this month two men came to my house and having great news asked me to close and lock my house. They had come from Homais, a fishing station about seven miles distant and on the open ocean. A vessel had been wrecked the night before. They had come all that distance to inform me, and the body of one of the sailors was now lifeless on shore before their fishing camp.

I made some necessary preparations and went out at once and was followed by a large number of the people from the Mission. It soon became evident that a great calamity had occurred. We had not walked more than three miles when we found a trunk full of ladies' dresses and children's wearing apparel on the beach. All along our road, which was over a beach covered with rocks and driftwood, we met signs of the disaster. When I arrived at Homais I found the body of the man covered with rocks. He had stripped and evidently tried to swim for shore. But the sea was so rough and the surroundings one vast mass of rocks, he had failed and drowned. There were no wounds on his body, save a scratch on his forehead. He seemed to be a man of twenty or thirty and had the complexion of a Scandinavian. We covered the body with canvas from the ship and dug a grave where I buried him.

Next I began to say my Vespers. The tide was going out so the Indians manned their canoes and went cruising amongst the rocks and in the small bays. All at once I heard a cry of alarm, and next I understood them to say that they had found the body of a woman. I went down to the landing just in time to take on shore the body of a young woman. She was evidently a lady of good circumstances, in all probability the Captain's wife. She was dressed very gorgeously and had likely put on all her best clothes, so as to save them, in case she should reach shore alive. I uncovered her face, over which the rescuers had drawn a veil. She had a small wound above the right eye. Otherwise she looked as

Captain E. Harlow, Mrs. A. Harlow and their two boys. All drowned when the bark *Malleville*, of Freeport, Maine, wrecked at Ho-me-is, near Estevan Point, October 1882.

if she were alive and in a trance. As I moved the body out of the canoe, I saw that her neck was broken. Her head swung from one side to the other, and with her beautiful blue eyes wide open I was almost tempted to believe that life was not gone. But she was dead — drowned with her husband and her two little boys. It was the saddest thing I ever saw in my life. The letter blocks of the children and their pet little pig were lying on the beach.

The vessel had gone to pieces and it was with some difficulty that I discovered that she was the bark *Malleville*, of Freeport, Me.—Captain E. Harlow. [27] The lady was Abbie Newcomb, of Brewster, Me., the young Captain's wife. I called upon the Chief of this clan and he supplied us with calico in which we wrapped the body of the lady. Then we got canvas off the vessel, made a shroud, and buried her near the grave of the sailor.

I must not forget to mention that the Indian who discovered the body and brought it on shore had taken from her hand two diamond and two gold rings—her wedding and engagement rings. He had also taken two diamond earrings, a gold pin and a piece of a gold watch chain — the watch having, in all probability, dropped into the sea. After landing the man gave me these articles of jewellery and asked me to take them in charge. I told this good fellow—who might be given as an example to civilized people for his honesty—that we would send them to the relatives of the lady. Altogether twenty-two people were drowned, including the second officer's wife.

After burying the dead and leaving instructions for the burial of some of the bodies which had not yet been recovered, I prepared to go home. I was sick at heart and completely exhausted with fatigue and hunger. I had passed two days with the most distressing scenes before me. I had seen, it is true, with satisfaction the noble and heroic work of the Indians. I had seen them up to their necks in the surf dragging the bodies to shore, those very people who at one time killed the living or left the dead unburied to become the prey of ravens or wolves. Yet my business on the inhospitable shore came vividly to mind as I saw the dead men, women and children before me — people who had relatives and for whom tears would be shed. That night I lay on a couple of planks placed by the Indians on the heads of two empty barrels, so I would be more or less protected against the vermin. A cold fever seized me. If it were not for the heat communicated by my dog, which I took as a bed-fellow, I would have perished of cold and misery.

On our way home we encountered the body of another sailor, an immense man dressed in blue overalls. The waves of the incoming tide moved the body in shore and with the half door cover of the hatch, we floated the corpse towards the beach. We began to lift them up, hatch door and corpse. We were thus proceeding when one of my men lost hold and the body went splashing back into the sea. It was dreadful. Finally we carried the unfortunate man to his last resting place. After digging a grave we let him sink into it and covered him with the hatch of the vessel on which he had met his sad end.

November 22. — A gunboat arrived in the harbour yesterday. The message which I sent to Victoria reached there by way of Alberni. Two young men volunteered to carry the news over the newly-built trail or road to the east coast and to Nanaimo. From there it reached the naval authorities.

Captain Thron of H.M.S. *King Fisher*, is now on his way back to Victoria with some of the details which he asked me to write for him. The arrival of this steamboat was a Godsend. I had lost the run of the days and could not say with certainty that we were keeping Sunday at a proper time or day. When, at one time, I was informed that one of our priests, Father Rondeault, had lost—or, rather gained a whole week and had given the ashes a week before Ash Wednesday, I thought such a mistake almost unpardonable. I know better now. It is a hint to me not to disbelieve the Indians when they report that they have kept Sunday on Monday or Saturday. I made the same mistake.

1883, January 30. — Upon the arrival of H.M.S. *King Fisher* in Victoria, dispatches were sent abroad with the news of the wreck. Today I received a letter from Mrs. Strout, of Portland, Me. The lady whom I buried was a relative of hers and she asked me to send the jewels to the dead lady's parents, who were living in Brewster, Me. From what I understand these people are Protestants, yet they believe in keeping relics of the dead. The letter was a beautiful one and exceedingly touching. Many were the thanks expressed by this estimable lady for the services rendered to her dead relative by the Indians and myself. Good Bishop Healy of Portland, Me., had given her permission to use his name in writing to me.

July 15. — Sent jewellery, Bible, and sealskin cloak to the mother of the late Mrs. Harlow, of Brewster. The Indians let me do so, although I could not promise any reward for their generous conduct and their trouble.

September. — At my request, the relatives of the shipwrecked people having neglected to reward the Indians, who had helped me bury the dead and had parted with the valuable jewellery, the American government granted a sum of two hundred dollars to be distributed among the most deserving ones. A gold medal was presented to Chief Aimé as a souvenir of the kindness and humane conduct of the tribe. The interest of the Mission and of the priest in charge were forgotten by all parties concerned.

December. — The Indians having commenced some of their winter festivals and the Chief being engaged in a *Klookwana*, a young woman fell into trances and began to prepare to become a medicine woman. As my position with the majority of the people was becoming solid, and as I could reckon upon being sustained in anything I would undertake for their good, I decided to interfere. Since the medicine men and women all sat around this candidate for new honours, I sent a posse of strong men to scatter them with menaces and threats. All the impostors immediately left the house and the young woman took to the bush. It is now settled that for the future consulting and employing medicine men and women can no longer be tolerated in this neighbourhood. Thus the greatest obstacle to the conversion of the Hesquiats is forever removed.

1884. — Bishop Brondel has gone to Montana to become Bishop there. Reverend Father Jouckau was to be his successor, but he did not accept on account of sickness and poor health. I hear that Archbishop Seghers has obtained permission to return to his old diocese.

"Manosaht" Indians and sailors from *H.M.S. King Fisher* at Refuge Cove, 1882.

August 15. — I had a narrow escape from drowning. I was coming from Nootka where I had spent a month. As I left Friendly Cove with a young man and his wife there was no wind, but a heavy sea was coming into Nootka Sound. It was a signal of the approach of a westerly wind. Just the wind we wanted. We had hardly travelled half a mile when we met the breeze, a regular gale. "What do you think of running for shore?" cried my Indian. "Take in sail, I cannot steer." I obeyed his orders. We were now in the midst of a fearful tempest. The woman began to cry and utter shrieks of despair. It was terrible, but I prayed like a good fellow. The sea was now breaking over our canoe ... I put the matter into the hands of St. Lawrence, whose feast we were to celebrate the next day. I called the reef, on which we happily succeeded in landing, St. Lawrence's reef. [28] The couple baled out the canoe and dried their blankets in the sun, and I retired amongst a little brushwood growing between the rocks. I made myself comfortable and slept the night.

September 9. — A wicked young fellow, the son of the most desperate character on the coast, had recourse to an old dodge, very frequently used in the past, to procure for himself a partner in life. A canoe of Nuchatlahts passed here and called at the village. The rascal watched his chance and whilst her friends were enjoying a hospitable meal in one of the houses, he went to their canoe and took by force a young woman, who struggled and cried as he carried her to his parent's residence. Although I felt inclined to stop the performance of this dastardly act, for motives of prudence I was compelled to abstain from interfering.

September 14. — Distant relatives of the young woman took her home to friends today.

Speaking in general, the people are orderly, docile and well-behaved.

Since the abolition of the medicine men and women free recourse is had to me for medicines and medical treatment. Day and night calls are made for remedies for the old and young. They want medicine for any and every complaint and there is no end to it. Strong burning medicines are preferred. In fact, mild remedies are discarded. Since last year I must have applied a square yard of blistering and mustard plasters to the aching limbs and bodies of my parishioners. I hope this habit of calling for help for even the most trivial ailments will soon cease. If not, I have a hard and busy time before me.

1885, November. — Since the beginning of last year the religious status of the tribe has greatly changed. Many adults have been baptized and received into the Church. All the marriages are now contracted in the Church and it is only a matter of time to have all the young people gather in the bosom of the Church. At last perseverance and prayer have carried the day. *Deo Gratias!*

Last June seventy young men went on a sealing expedition to the Bering Sea. They did very well, and arrived home highly delighted with the success of their long voyage. They had killed 1400 animals, receiving two dollars per animal. However, their earnings were considerably reduced, as they had to pay for their board on the vessel. Their mode of hunting is as follows. Their canoes are taken on board the vessel and secured on deck. When they come to the Sea their canoes are lowered. Then the men, with spears and some provisions and a compass, begin to cruise around, hunting. They return to the vessel to spend the night.

It is hazardous work, as the waters of the Bering Sea are very treacherous and become covered with a dense fog, sometimes more than once a day. The Indians use their compass, but it takes good reckoning to come from a distance of ten or fifteen miles to the spot where the vessel is drifting. In such weather signal guns are fired and are of great assistance to the befogged hunters. On their first voyage two men lost their vessel and by their absence on board caused much uneasiness and grief to their friends and many tears to their relatives at home on the arrival of the schooner. They are now back, and pose as heroes. After

H.M.S. Boxer at anchor, Friendly Cove, Nootka Sound, ca. 1879.

101

losing the vessel they landed on one of the Aleutian Islands. There they met a native who treated them well and, by signs and gestures, showed them the direction of a trading post. The trader, a white man, gave them some provisions and directed them to a bay where American fishermen were busy at their trade. Thence they were taken in a boat and landed at one of the central trading stations. They were then taken to San Francisco on the Alaska Commercial Company's steamer *Dorah.*

They were treated with much kindness by the Captain and his men. The first officer took the two men, bewildered upon seeing the large city, to the British Consul, who paid their passages to Victoria. There they at once went over to see the Bishop, who assisted them by a letter of recommendation to the owners of the vessel from which they had strayed. A canoe was bought and a supply of provisions and they arrived home last Sunday, just in time to attend Mass. They now excite the wonder of all the Indians. No doubt their experiences, told in all detail, would excite the admiration of people more accustomed to travel than these Indians who had never before left their home and country.

Wewiks, the son of parents whose great pride it was to entertain the tribe with food and presents, while only half feeding and clothing their own children, got in trouble and died a few weeks ago. It has been stormy and dangerous-looking for me ever since. I now have a paper on my table stating that, if I do not turn up and that my body is found with evidence of having been murdered, traces of it can be found on the lower limbs of the man who committed the deed. I have, since the beginning of this trouble, carried a revolver with the object of wounding in the lower limbs the man who committed the assault. Then nobody but the guilty party may be hauled up.

Wewiks broke into the store of a trader. He was condemned to six months imprisonment, contracted consumption in prison and died a week after his return home. Three days before his death his father came to my house and began to abuse and threaten me. I took it calmly and simply cast the blame on the boy who had broken into the store. Just before leaving me the old man changed his tone and gave me to understand that my services as a priest would not be rejected. So I went over and prepared the poor young fellow for death. The sick man had in his possession a brand new gun. It was lying alongside his bed. What was the use of his parents buying a gun, when it was evident that their boy must soon die? And was the bed of the dying man the proper place to keep the dangerous weapon? Such remarks and hints as these were thrown out to me. I could easily see that my position was not a safe one.

The evening before the young fellow died, a messenger, the sick boy's brother, came to ask me to go over to the house. It was dark, the Indians had retired for the night and the sick man was dying in a house away from the settlement. He had no company save his wicked parents. A coasting trader was with me when the invitation was made. He jumped up as I rose to follow the messenger and entreated me not to go, that they were going to kill me. The last words I heard him call out being, "Oh, Father, come back. For God's sake do not go."

I knew that I was running a great risk, but how could I in conscience refuse to go and see a dying man? On my way I called on a man whom I could trust, and asked him to accompany me. How disappointed the sick man's parents looked when they saw that I was not alone. My presence as a priest was not wanted. Not one of them spoke a word to me, but they all entered in conversation with my companion. After a while I returned to my house with the consolation that I had done my duty.

Wewiks died, but his people objected to having him buried from the church. They were bent on making trouble. His body was placed on the branches of a huge tree, covered and decorated with blankets. The famous gun was also in evidence as an ornament.

March 1886 — For the first time in the history of the world Confirmation was administered on this coast. On the 28th of February, the Most Reverend C.J. Seghers, Archbishop of Vancouver, administered here in the Church of Hesquiat. The sacrament was given to thirty-seven adults.

On the occasion of his visit to the coast, the Bishop went to Kyuquot, where I accompanied him with Father Lemmens. We went on a schooner and were well received by the Kyuquots, who had been duly prepared by their priest, Father Nicolaye. The Bishop on this occasion blessed the cemetery at Kyuquot. Then we returned in a canoe and visited the different tribes on our way home, preached to the people and baptized their children. We came near to being drowned near Bajo Point, but escaped as by a miracle. We made our home in Friendly Cove for a week, on account of bad weather. At last we managed to reach Hesquiat and enjoy a full if not a luxurious meal.

After the Bishop's departure, the next news which I received was that Father Lemmens was stationed in Clayoquot Sound and that my work was reduced to looking after the Hesquiat, Nootka and Muchalat Indians.

1887. — On the occasion of his last visit the Bishop had made arrangements for building a new dwelling house, my old quarters having become almost uninhabitable. We therefore commenced work early in June. I had logs squared and ready for the carpenters on their arrival and the foundations laid. The house was to be of logs with lining inside and rustic outside. The two white men employed did their best, but understood very little about building a log house. It took more time than we expected and was much more costly.

While this was going on Archbishop Seghers was absent in Alaska. We were overwhelmed with grief when we learned in August that he had been murdered. The news was so unexpected and of such an unheard-of nature that my men dropped their tools in complete discouragement. We had no details, but that the Bishop was dead. The news utterly upset us.

Most of my people were absent. They had been induced to leave their homes and to go to the hop fields near Puget Sound. The news of the death of our lamented Bishop came almost simultaneously with the news of sickness amongst the thousands of Indians who were in the hop fields. Later on some of the people began to come home. Their children had died of measles. Others brought their little ones home, but they had

Clayoquot Village, Stubbs Island, Clayoquot Sound.

104

the sickness with them. Having been exposed to the cold in their canoes, many died and those who seemed to have recovered became consumptive and soon followed the others to the grave. Before long I counted over forty children of Hesquiat alone who had become victims of the disease. With my Bishop murdered and my young people dying around me, I closed this year with many, many sad feelings.

August 17, 1888. — Today I received word through the wife of the Indian agent for the coast that a murder had been committed at Hesquiat. The body of a little boy of four years had been found behind one of the houses. There was no evidence to prove by whom he had been killed. This news spoiled all the pleasure and enjoyment of my presence at the consecration of Bishop Lemmens. I went home with a crew of Indians who had specially come for me. It was a long, tedious trip, all the more unpleasant as I could see the trouble I had before me on account of the murder.

Harry Guillod, Indian Agent, West Coast Agency, 1884-1903.

August 21. — I arrived home shortly before midnight and retired at once. About two a.m. I heard somebody knock at the door. I waited for another knock, but the visitor left. Early next morning a man called Isiniquah came to see me. He began to say that he was falsely accused of being the murderer, but I would not give him a hearing. Later in the evening he came again and asked me what the Indians had been telling me about him. Again I sent him off without making any statement.

The Indian agent called a couple of days later and went to Victoria to inform the authorities of the circumstances of the crime. A magistrate and a couple of policemen were sent. Isiniquah underwent a preliminary hearing and was taken to civilization for trial. [29]

Meanwhile the father of the murdered child arrived home from the Bering Sea. I never in my life saw a man the victim of such a struggle to control his temper. However, he held out. I heard him say to his weeping wife, "Now let us not be over-sad. If we are good we will see our little boy again in Heaven." The tears came to my eyes and it struck me then that if I had had my troubles, I had at least done some good by remaining and trying to do my duty.

October 25. — The schooner *Kate* arrived here and had been chartered by the government to take the witnesses to Nanaimo for the trial of Isiniquah. I received a summons to accompany them and act as interpreter. I did, rather than pay a fine of five hundred dollars for non-attendance.

The trial came off in due time. It lasted three days and Isiniquah was condemned to be hanged December 12th. The Methodist ministers and one Presbyterian bigot got up a petition to have the sentence commuted, or rather, have the prisoner discharged. They consider it a piece of persecution and compared the proceedings to the proceedings of the Spanish Inquisition. The object at the bottom was to gain the good-will of the natives who were related to the murderer, thus preparing the field for a Protestant mission on the coast. This was the first attempt they made to intrude on our missions.

December 19. — Isiniquah was hanged on December 12th, after being duly prepared by baptism and instruction in our holy religion.

The motive for his crime had been, presumably, the fact that one of his children, who had died of measles, was called Moses. The boy he had killed had the French name Moise. This boy was the son of Michel, a good Christian. Isiniquah and his friends, according to an old pagan custom, wanted Michel to give another name to his child on account of the similarity of the names. Michel having refused to do so, the murderer availed himself of the absence of the parent and the

106

grandfather of the boy to get him out of the way. He unmercifully took the little fellow in the bush, put his hand firmly on the mouth and nostrils of the child then choked him to death. When the sentence was pronounced in court, a white Catholic woman, the mother of several little children was heard to say, "A rope is too good to hang a man who has choked to death an innocent child."

When the time for going back to the Mission arrived, the government put at our disposition the schooner *Favorite* Captain L. McLean. The Indians took along a supply of building lumber and other material with the object of improving their habitations and their mode of living. I had on board several thousand feet of lumber and bricks for a new church in Friendly Cove.

After discharging men and freight at Hesquiat, at the request of the Captain, I returned on board. We started on December 17th, about noon. The wind was favourable but there was considerable sea on and the weather looked bad. In less than two hours we were sailing into the Sound. As we neared Friendly Cove the wind abated and soon began to blow against us.

It was now dark and the wind shifted again, favourably this time. I was down below when the Captain came down to put on his mackintosh and asked me to follow him on deck. He wanted me to act as interpreter. There were two Indians on board who he could not understand, but, being of the district, he wanted them to act as pilots. The Captain had been in Friendly Cove only once before. The weather now being thick, he was not sure that he could make the harbour. The rain fell in torrents and the wind blew a hurricane. I now stood against the mainmast and the Indians were giving their orders, which I interpreted. The skipper had his misgivings about the directions, but he followed them. The Indians knew the entrance of Friendly Cove...Yes, that was the cove. But it was not the Cove...it was a small bay close to the entrance of the real harbour. The *Favorite*, having sailed in at full speed, was before long going to be in extreme danger on the rocky shore. The would-be pilots were despondent. The skipper kept cool and ordered his sailors to run lines on shore. They were to fasten them to the rocks and then try to keep the vessel from going to pieces. I heard the skipper make only one sour remark and he did so in his solemn, stern way. "I could shoot those sons of savages as they stand in their boots." His mistake was that they wore no boots.

The sailors, after fastening lines to the rocks to keep the vessel from striking, came back on board and began to put their clothes and belongings in their traps and bags to have them ready when ordered to

107

abandon the vessel. As for myself, I was advised by the kind captain to turn in, if I wanted a couple of hours rest. How could I, with my shoes full of water while on the vessel that might go to pieces at any time?

That night was a dreary one for us all, as the vessel began to roll on the rocks and keeled over considerable. Early in the morning, as the tide came in, she slid down from the boulders. Finally she was afloat again. The men, later in the day, hauled her out from her dangerous position and anchored her in Friendly Cove. She was damaged very noticeably and from the very start she took in quite a bit of water. The next six days were spent in the Cove — about the most dreary days I have spent in this worldly sphere. There were no Indians around, the weather was bad and everyone seemed dejected and downcast.

We made a start for home on Friday—a week since we had entered Nootka Sound. A light, northerly breeze was blowing, hardly strong enough to move out of the channel. When the everlasting easterly, the *Toochi*, sprang up, it favoured us for a time. At four p.m. we were off Hole in the Wall, at the mouth of the great harbour. But the weather looked thick and the captain determined to "lay to" that night.

As soon as the vessel began to roll, her pumps were called into service every fifteen minutes and an amount of water came forth each time.

Friendly Cove Village.

108

Meanwhile the *Favorite* was drifting southwest. The wind increased as the night advanced and about ten the Second Mate came down, drenched with rain, and reported, for my consolation, that we were drifting to the southwest like a "bundle of straw". Later, at the shift of the sailors' watch, I overheard a secret conversation which was to the effect that, if they ever got into port, the sailors would abandon the vessel and get to town the best way they could, rather than stay on the leaking craft. Further details would be superfluous. Suffice to say that for a whole week we were in a continuation of gales of wind and rain. The sailors were at the pumps day and night. The waves rolled right over the vessel. At last a westerly wind came to our assistance. Land was sighted and after sailing a full day before the wind we at last cast anchor at Hesquiat. According to our Captain's reckoning we had been blown a hundred miles from shore and out of our course.

Close of 1888. — There are now in Hesquiat only three or four families of real pagan Indians. The rest of the settlement are Christians—some of them very fervent, the others less so.

1889, May. — The old chief Townissim, the father of Matlahaw, died here the other day. The old man had a better chance than his son, who had died unbaptized and impenitent, to meet his Maker and Judge. For several years he had been a regular attendant at church, and was baptized and received all the rites of the Church before his death. R.I.P.

August. — I built a new chapel in Friendly Cove.

1890. — I saw the Nootka Indians, stayed with them a short time and then went on a voyage to Europe — the first since my arrival in the country twenty-one years ago.

November. — I returned from the old country, where I had spent four months, and secured the necessary funds for a new church in Hesquiat. It was about time to move out of the old building, for it had become a complete wreck. It rained on my head as I was saying Mass, and the floor of the building was covered with water. It was the poorest church in Christendom.

1891, March. — Two French Canadian carpenters arrived here last month on the schooner *Favorite*, loaded with building material. On account of the general boom in British Columbia the wages are very high, my men being paid three dollars and fifty cents per day. The plan of the new church was made by Stephen Donovan, of Victoria, but was considerably modified on account of the lack of means to put up a building such as he had designed.

October. — I understand that a young man representing the Presbyterian Church of Canada has taken up his residence at Alberni.

1892, July. — There is a great excitement here, and the old pagan people are exceedingly provoking. It was known all along the coast that Antoin, the young Chief, was sick and sinking fast of consumption. The young man, a good lad, was preparing for death as a Christian. Now the chiefs from the neighbourhood sent medicine men and women to tempt him and make him renounce Christianity. All their efforts were of no avail. The young Chief died after receiving the last rites of the Church. Being defeated in this matter they insisted that his house should be broken down and burned. This was always done in the case of anybody dying childless, especially if the departed was a chief. At first I objected, but as the aunt was willing to allow the movers to have their own way, I withdrew my opposition. And so Antoin's house, which he had built and intended to occupy as soon as he was married, was torn down and burned on the beach. The Hesquiats have no chief again. The aunt of the departed will now be regent until her infant son becomes of age.

February 1893. — The Right Reverend Bishop Lemmens paid his first visit to the Indians of this district. As a piece of bad news the Bishop told me that the Methodists were preparing to put up a mission in Nitinat and had obtained a grant of five hundred dollars from the Dominion government for missionary purposes. They had asked for and obtained the grant for the building of a school. Of course with them that means a meeting-house or a church.

December. — My people this year have had considerable sickness in

Nootka Mission.

110

the village and many deaths have occurred. It casts a gloom over the place. Otherwise the outlook is good.

July 1894. — During my absence a party of Indians from the state of Washington came across the Straits with a supply of whiskey which they intended to dispose of in Hesquiat. As soon as the presence of the liquor in the settlement became known, three of my Christian Indians went and took it away and secreted it in one of the rooms of my house. I reported this to the Indian Department and the men who had acted so judiciously in confiscating the vile spirits received each a reward of twenty dollars from the Dominion government.

Very touching stories reached us from Nootka. The Indians of that district, having refused my services as a priest for a long time, are not as well instructed as they might have been. They were not of real bad will, but the Chief having lost his only child the whole tribe went into mourning, the consequence being that they excluded not only their games but also the practice of religion.

One of their young men, having been sick a very long time and feeling that his end was coming, sent for his nearest relatives. This is usual with all the people and the scenes that are then enacted are sometimes most touching.

The patient is duly prepared for the arrival of the visitors. One comes in after the other, the men stoically, the women with a sad face and weeping voice. When they are all seated they all begin to cry and lament and wail. The noise which they make, as they all join in the songs of grief, must be a torture to the dying relative. But it is a matter of pride and deep consolation to the living when not only near and distant relatives call, but especially if the Chief and his subjects related to the patient extend a visit. After death it is always remembered who did and who did not call. The feeling of the living is good or bad towards their neighbours in accordance with the fact that they have or have not performed this act of etiquette.

In this present case the poor young fellow, being now left alone with his mother, his step-father, and a half-brother, gave orders to count the money which he had still left. He had been a great sea otter hunter and very successful, especially the last season. He then sent his half-brother for a suit of new clothes which he put on — the Indians always put on to the dying their best clothes and blankets. Then he sent for another another suit and underclothes. The trader told me that he spent over one hundred dollars for wearing apparel in his place, and the orders of the dying man were that what he could not put on should be enclosed in the coffin or box in which his body was put for burial.

111

It is a very curious custom, but in most cases the coffin contains not only the body, but also a great many things dear to the dead one, such as clothes, toys and money. His favourite dog is killed, his canoe split up, his watch or clock destroyed. Anything and everything that would remind the living of the dead is done away with and gotten out of sight. As noticed already, articles or parts of articles having belonged to an enemy are also very often enclosed with the body, the idea and belief being that such a proceeding will have the effect of causing sickness and death to an adversary.

The other case referred to was that of a young man whose two little children had died before him. He evidently expected to join them in the next world, for shortly before his death he sent a messenger to the nearest trading station with orders to buy such and such toys, at one time dear to his little ones. He ordered them placed in his coffin with his own body the moment his death should occur.

This was an old practice. The fact that it existed before the arrival of a priest on this coast proves that the natives believed in a life after this life. Were they not ahead of some of our civilized would-be scientists?

1895. — Our Indians over all the coast are well-disposed. This being known seems to have excited the Presbyterian and Methodist denominations. Their efforts to invade the coast are very pronounced. A monthly steamer now visits the coast, as the government has established a Scandinavian settlement at Cape Scott at the northern end of the Island, and bound itself to carry the mails and provisions once a month. With these facilities of travel and the peaceful behaviour of the natives all along the coast, the zeal of the Protestant ministers has grown to the extent that they now have established themselves at different points on the coast. When a man's life was in danger and when the only means of travelling was an Indian canoe, when the mails reached us only once or twice a year ... we were welcome to do alone the work of converting the natives. Now with the present facilities and the absence of danger, the ministers come in sight to give us trouble and pervert our Indian children.

After mature reflection I made up my mind to propose to our Bishop a plan for his approbation. I would build, in a central part of the coast, an industrial school for boys and girls.

August. — We had a retreat for the clergy last month. Before returning I spoke to the Bishop of the idea of a boarding school. His Lordship called on the Indian agent, who promised that he would obtain a grant for the support of the teachers and children from the Dominion government. Next I was sent for and this same agent urged me to put up the buildings at once, and said that as soon as the school was occupied a per capita grant would be available.

Everything we asked for was promised by the agent. I returned to my Mission rejoicing in the thought that the efforts of the Protestant ministers would be unsuccessful. If we could keep the children from perversions, our position was safe.

I am now sorry to put on record that, per letter from the head of our diocese, I was yesterday informed that I must abandon the idea of having a boarding school which, in my mind, is the only means to save the fruits of my labours of more than twenty years. I must submit and be resigned to the regulations of the one who rules over me—my Bishop.

1896. — A young man representing the Presbyterian Church is now stationed in Ahousat. [30] He is a school teacher by profession, but he holds divine service on Sunday. He established himself between two missions having a resident priest. He will do nothing himself, but he will report, as a credit to himself, any improvements these Indians will make. Yet all the credit will belong to the example of my people in Hesquiat and the Clayoquot tribe. And the poor little children so anxious to learn to read and write will be perverted without noticing it.

1897. — News has reached me that Bishop Lemmens died in Guatemala. So then we are again without a Bishop. It is reported that he died of the fever of that swampy country. He had gone there to collect funds for his new cathedral in Victoria. R.I.P. [31]

1898, February. — This year opened with sickness in the settlement. Whooping cough was brought here by a family of visiting strangers. They were here for several days and their children having the cough communicated the dreaded disease to our children. I have my hands full just now.

February 15. — Today, after a spell of vain-glory, I feel terribly disappointed. The night before last I was called out about midnight to visit the child of a young couple. They wanted medical treatment for the coughing infant. It was a dark night but the sky was cloudless. So I took my lantern, whistled for my dog and wended my way in the direction of the village. I noticed a light in some of the houses, for there was sickness in almost all of them. The wolves were howling in the distance, and the Indian dogs were barking at the rising moon. The sea was breaking against the shore, but there was not a human soul to break the solemnity, and the monotony of the midnight hour. Oh, what a wild, lonely country this is after all. In the home I was impatiently expected ... the child was very bad; the chest and lungs very much affected. I administered the usual remedies and returned home with the expectation of having another funeral. Yesterday I went over again. My patient was very much better and likely to recover. This made me feel good and the thought of vain-glory got the best of me. Today the child is dead. I went to the church this morning to ring my bell for Mass and found under the bell tower a small box containing all that was mortal of the dear little child whom yesterday I prided myself of having treated and restored to health.

April. — I lost a few days ago one of the most sensible and most pious persons it has been my fortune to have in my parish. This woman for several years refused to become a Christian. Her reason was the fact that she was afraid that she might be tempted and return to the old pagan practices. She was converted at last. From the day of her reception in the Church by baptism, she attended Mass every day of the week and was at church every Sunday twice. Her last message to her family was to remain faithful to, and follow the instructions of, the priest. She was buried on Sunday morning at the parochial Mass. Her husband said the prayers aloud, to which the rest of the people answered. I attempted to say a few words, but the sadness in the church was such that I broke down and cried with the rest.

August. — Bishop Christie was consecrated in St. Paul, Minn., June 29th and arrived in his new diocese on the 5th of August. With new courage and the prospects of an early visit to our missions by the new prelate, I returned to Hesquiat and began at once to prepare some of my people for Confirmation.

1899. — I received a letter from Bishop Christie with this message, "Come to Victoria at once. I want to consult with you about building a boarding school for the Indian children of the west coast. I have just returned from Ottawa and have obtained a per capita grant from the government for fifty children. If we do not accept the grant it will be given to one of the sects. Your children will be perverted and you will lose the fruit of all your labours."

In Victoria the good Bishop explained all his plans; "But", he said, "Father, we have no money to do the work. However, let us commence at once. *Deus providebit*. Return to the coast at the first opportunity, choose a central location and I will send up lumber and men to do the work."

At the foot of a mountain in Deception Channel I found and secured a large piece of table-land open to pre-emption and away from all the Indian settlements. It is fifty feet above the surface of a fine bay which at low water has a sandy beach of more than twenty acres—a magnificent playground for children. It is also in proximity to another bay, a real clamfield, so that with a bay swarming with salmon and other fish, the expense of supporting the children will be considerably reduced and their health will be benefitted. All our people from their very infancy look upon fish as their main food. They acknowledge that without fish they cannot live and keep their health.

A few days later I received another letter from Bishop Christie, announcing that he was to leave us and go to Portland, Oregon, as the successor of Archbishop Gross. The Archbishop-elect now told me again to go ahead with the work, insisting that if the school was not built now it would never be built. Either the Methodists or the Presbyterians would get our grant and use it to pervert our Catholic children. In the course of conversation afterwards His Grace told me that he had talked the matter over with his Vicar-General. They had come to the conclusion that as soon as the work was well started I should go abroad to collect the necessary funds. "And," he said, "Father, let us go ahead. The work of your life will be destroyed. It will be lost if we neglect this chance offered by the government. We must put up the buildings and pay for them ourselves. But the Indian Department will, by a generous yearly grant, do the rest. When the

Father Brabant's dream — the Christie Indian School.

115

buildings are up, you will have to go East and ask the good people out there to extend to us a helping hand. And, Father, do not be uneasy. You will do well. The people out there do not know what you are doing for the salvation of souls. I had no idea of it myself before coming here.''

October. — Our school is now built ...

NOTES

1. The eighteen tribes were the Checkleset, Kyuquot, Ehatisat, Nuchatlat, Muchalat, Moachat, Hesquiat, Ahousat, Kelsemat, Clayoquot, Ucluelet, Toquat, Uchucklisat, Hopachisat, Tsishaat, Ohiat, Nitinat and Pachenat.
2. Brabant somewhat exaggerates his isolation. There were light-keepers at the Cape Beale Lighthouse, a settlement at Sooke and homesteads at least as far north as the Jordan River area. As early as 1861 there were five trading posts in Barkley Sound. An 1892 directory lists John Margovitch as the manager of a store at Hesquiat.
3. For a detailed account of the Spanish at Nootka see Jose Mariano Mozino's *Noticias de Nutka.* Escalante Reef may have been named after one of the Spanish friars.
4. Densmore appears to agree with this theory.
5. Captain William Spring, with Captain Hugh McKay, began trading on the northwest coast in the 1850's. During much of the author's time on the coast, McKay and Spring, or Spring and Co., seem to have had a monopoly.
6. The Cape Beale Light was in operation by June of 1874. The first lightkeepers were R. Westmoreland and Thomas Woods.
7. Keeshan is perhaps better known as Execution Rock. See Scott's *Barkley Sound.* He writes of the Indian legends associated with the rock, with exceptional insight.
8. Lang or Laing.
9. Chinook, although Brabant never mentions it, was the trading jargon of the west coast. For many years Brabant conversed and preached in Chinook.
10. A *rancherie* is an Indian village or settlement. In California it meant the people living off the ranch; in Russian Alaska it seems to have meant the village outside of a stockade.
11. *Tsiekas.* I have been unable to trace or define this word.
12. Fort Rupert is not to be confused with Prince Rupert. The fort was abandoned in 1852. Today Port Hardy occupies the location of Fort Rupert.
13. The road wasn't "newly-made", but it had obviously been cleared out prior to the author's trip. No one seems to know when this road was made. In all likelihood it was originally an Indian trading trail.

14. *Leplet* is Chinook for priest.
15. *Memaloose* is the Chinook word for death.
16. Nicholson quotes the following extracts from Brabant's "few words":

My Lord — sad news — I am shot in the right hand and in the back. Please get a priest at once. I may get well if a doctor comes at once to extract the shot.

My Lord — I am dying. Adieu. Pray for me.

My Lord — inflammation is setting in my hand. The Indians are very kind. The whole tribe is crying night and day. At least three are taking care of me. Do not blame them. Praise their kindness, and may another priest be soon here to take my place — is the wish of Your Lordship's dying servant.

17. The *Pacific* collided with the *Orpheus* off shore during the night of November 4, 1874. Of the 250 passengers on the *Pacific* only two survived.
18. I have been unable to trace the word *Okhei*. Densmore speaks of the ceremony, but does not mention a title. In her version the visitors are women. Brabant and Densmore do agree however on the presentation of gifts and the following feast.
19. Maquinna died at Friendly Cove, 1902.
20. According to Father Nicolaye, writing in 1914, the Indians did not find Matlahaw's body. Archbishop Seghers and Fathers Brabant and Nicolaye found the body in 1876 while looking for a more suitable location for the Mission.
21. This "ghost" may have been Nicholson's Ahoots-oos (p. 270.) More likely it was a localized legend.
22. *Osemitch* or *Osumitch*, "the Clayoquot term for the process of purifying the body by washing and rubbing with hemlock sprigs, in order to obtain special ability from supernatural beings." Curtis, p. 46
23. *Haweim* is obviously the "Great Chief" of the Nootkans. *Kwayetsim* is probably *Kwatyat*, a cultural hero. *We'a Kawaitliume, Wawittillsois* and *Wakouix*, may be local variants of "Father Daylight" to whom the Nootkans generally address their prayers.
24. *Way tribes*. There is no tribe by this name. It is impossible to tell just whom Brabant is referring to.
25. *Heitlik* is the giant snake of Nootkan mythology.
26. The *Klookwana* is the great winter ceremony of the Nootkans. It also can mean the shaman (Loqwona), or the Shaman's Dance.
27. The *Malleville* broke up on Perez Rock. Brabant found only eight bodies. The author implies that he walked the beach; Nicholson claims that he walked eight miles on the overland trail. In another place Brabant writes 5 miles and eleven people.
28. In all probability St. Lawrence's Reef is now the Lawrence Island group.

117

29. The authorities spelled the murderer's name as Isinchwan. Indians were executed at Hesquiat in 1869 for murdering the survivors of the *John Bright*, which was wrecked on Boulder Point in February of that year. The tribes of the area were brought to Hesquiat to watch the executions.
30. The "young man" was the Reverend Melvin Swartout who worked out of Ucluelet from 1894 until he drowned at Florencia Bay in 1904.
31. It is odd that Brabant fails to mention the burning of his church in 1897 and the wreck of the *S.S. Cleveland*. The six men who finally made it to Hesquiat after the wreck repayed the author's hospitality by rebuilding his church.

BIBLIOGRAPHY

Bird, George H.   1971. *Tse-ees-tah* [*One Man in a Boat*].
Arrowsmith Press Ltd., Port Alberni.

Curtis, Edward.   1916. *The North American Indian.*
Johnson Reprint Corporation, New York.

Densmore, Frances.   1939. *Nootka and Quileute Music.*
United States Government Printing Office,
Washington.

Drucker, Philip.   1951. *The Northern and Central Nootkan Tribes.*
United States Government Printing Office,
Washington.

Duff, Wilson.   1964. *The Impact of the White Man.*
Anthropology in British Columbia Memoir
No. 5, Victoria.

Geographic Board of   1913. *Handbook of Indians of Canada.*
Canada.   The King's Printers, Ottawa.

Koppert, V.A.   1930. *Contributions to Clayoquot Ethnology.*
The Catholic University of America,
Anthropological Series No. 1, Washington.

Moser, Reverend Chas.   1926. *Reminiscences of the West Coast of*
Vancouver Island.
The Acme Press, Ltd., Victoria.

Mozino, Jose Mariano.   1970. *Noticias de Nutka.*
McClelland and Stewart, Ltd., Toronto.

Nicholson, George.   1973. *Vancouver Island's West Coast.*
George Nicholson, Victoria.

Provincial Archives.   1966. *Nootka.*
Department of Education, Victoria.

Sapir, Edward and   1955. *Native Accounts of Nootka Ethnology.*
Swadesh, Morris.   Indiana University, Bloomington.

Scott, Bruce R.   1970. *"Breakers Ahead!"*
Review Publishing House, Sidney.

—————.   1972. *Barkley Sound.*
Fleming-Review Printing Ltd., Victoria.

Van Der Heyden,   1920. *Life and Letters of Father Brabant.*
Reverend Joseph.   J. Wouters-Ickx, Louvain.

INDEX

Acous 19
Ahousaht tribe 17-18, 49
Ahousat (place) 79, 89-90, 113
Aktese 18, 81
Alberni Canal 33
Alert (schooner) 13, 14, 60
Anna Beck (schooner) 71

Becher Bay 13
Bokshis Inlet 27
H.M.S. Boxer 24, 26-27, 101
Brondel, Bishop 84-86, 99
Brown, Captain George 34-35, 60

Canoes, building 60
Checkleset tribe 18-20, 37, 58
Cheeshish 21
Chickluat 27
China River 33
Christianson, Captain J. 13
Christie, Bishop 114-16
Clayoquot Inlet 30
Clayoquot tribe 16, 30-31
Collins, Captain 26-27

Donovan, Stephan 109
Dorah (steamer) 102

Edwin (bark) 35
Ehattesaht tribe 21, 58
Ehchachist 16
Ekool 32-34
Ekoolthaht tribe 32, 52-53
Emma (steamer) 33
Etawinni 28

Favorite (schooner) 13-14, 71, 107-09
Florencia Bay 31
Francis, Captain Peter 13, 21, 23-24
Friendly Cove 10, 22, 26-27, 103, 107-09

Guillod, Harry 105

Harlow, Captain E. 96-97
Harris, Captain 45
Hoiss 28
Homais 26
Hot Springs Cove 25
Hughes, Captain 35

Indian School 114-16

Jouckau, Reverend Father 99

Kate (schooner) 107
Keeshan 15
Kelsemaht tribe 17
H.M.S. King Fisher 98
Klookwana (Indian ceremony) 87-89
Koninnah 49-50
Kyuquot 20, 27, 38, 103
Kyuquot tribe 18-20, 80-81, 103

Lang, Andrew 15
Leclaire, Noel 34, 37
Lemmens, Reverend Father 103
  Right Reverend 110, 113

McClean, Captain L. 107-09
McKay, Captain Hugh 13, 71

Malleville (bark) 95-98
Man-of-War Harbour 27
Maquinna 29, 58
Marktosis 46
Marriage, Indian 75-78
Matlahaw 34-36, 40-42, 59
Moos, Neils 24
Morrin 71-72
Muchalat tribe 21, 28

Namukamis 32, 65-66, 71-72, 78-79
Nanaimo 33
Newcomb, Abbie 95-97
Nicolaye, Reverend Father, P. J. 60, 62,
  70-73, 78-79, 86, 103
Nootka tribe 28, 38
Nuchatlaht 28
Nuchatlaht tribe 20, 21

Ohiet tribe 24, 65-66, 78
Ois 28
Opetchesahts 33
Opitsat 24
Osemitch (Indian ceremony) 66-67

Pacific (steamship) 45-46
Peterson, John 13, 20
Port San Juan 13-14
Potlatch 53-55
Powell, Dr. 24, 26

Redfern, Dr. 45
H.M.S. Rocket 45
Rondeault, Reverend Father 34, 37

Scanlan, Tim 25-27
Sealing 101-02
Sea Otters 94-95
Seddall Island 16
Seektukis 24, 29
Seghers, Right Reverend Charles 13-14,
  16-17, 19-20, 23, 27, 29-34, 38, 44-45,
  60, 79, 99, 103-04
Sheouse, Chief 39
Sheshaht tribe 33
Shiyous 29-30
Sitakenin 16, 30
Smallpox 38-42, 45
Sorcerers 81-84
Spring, Captain W. 13, 21
Spring and Company 13, 24
St. Leo's Mission 71-72, 79
Surprise (schooner) 13-14, 18, 20-21,
  24, 38

Tahsis 28
Thornberg, Fred 43
Thornton, Captain 32
Thornton (sloop) 34
Thron, Captain 98
Townissim 40-41, 59, 69, 109

Uchuklesaht tribe 22
Ucluelet 15, 30-32
Ucluelet tribe 15

Walken, Dr. 44
Warren, Captain Douglas 36, 71
Warren and Company 16, 34
Wish Koutl 15, 32